Stuart Watkins was k  in the Chinese Year London, Berkshire ar Levels and a Special read Chemistry at Wo successful career in ...ஸ் management. This was abruptly cut short by an acute psychotic episode in Norwich in 1994, which developed into chronic schizophrenia which he is still afflicted with. He suffered a cerebellar stroke in 2009.

He is a Capricorn, has a 28-year-old son, and lives in Yorkshire.

ISBN 13: 9781793869005

'A United Kingdom'

Trains of Logical Thought

(Exercises in Critical Thinking)

Dedications & Acknowledgements

My heartfelt thanks to Sarah Laurel for her help with the visuals. The project would have been impossible without her invaluable ideas, advice, input and technical prowess.

I would like to dedicate this piece of work to my parents, who have led me by their example in tackling and defeating all obstacles in their path. My fights against horrific mental demons, as well as my physical ailments, have been bolstered by their wind at my back, and also my son Troy and my partner in crime - and my inspiration - Sarah. Without them all I would, without a shred of doubt, have left this beautiful Earth many moons before now.

Having suffered with schizophrenia for almost 25 years now, and the periods of abject darkness it sometimes brings with it, and also in consideration of the "time-bombs" I refer to within **Pandora's Box**, I will be donating 10% of any profits to the mental health charity MIND.

I apologise to everybody that I have mistreated in my life; there are a great many more of you than I would have chosen, if the choice had been mine to make. You all know who you are.

Stuart

'A United Kingdom'

Trains of Logical Thought

CONTENTS

Introduction

My perspective on some issues affecting Britain, the so-called United Kingdom.

I am a socialist, a feminist, an atheist, a real democrat (small 'd'), a real republican (small 'r', opposer of the monarchy), a spiritualist, a humanist, a passionate supporter of the NHS, Jeremy Corbyn and the LGBTQ+ community, a pacifist, and a proud European.

I am an opponent of corruption in all its forms, of oppression in all its forms, of the Conservative Party and their cruel ideology, the Right Wing Press, racism, sexism, ageism, (all "-isms"), inequality, elites and unearned privilege, and the unaccountability of individuals, publications and institutions.

I have been accused at times of being opinionated, arrogant and judgemental, and I am, without doubt, guilty as charged. But I would not have been able to produce this material without all three of those traits. Many people could of course be described by the same words, and perhaps some of them get a mention. In any case, there are a lot more facts and sound logic in here than just opinions.

I believe robustly in every single word of this - but I would probably prefer to have read it as the output of someone else. Nobody else wrote it though, and I didn't, in the end, have any choice in the matter. There was just too much that needed to be said.

I am not a TV personality, celebrity, or published intellectual or recognised expert, and so it is highly likely that I will have to publish and promote this book by myself; I am neither a famous chef putting out my twenty-fifth book of hotpot recipes, nor am I a sixty-year old politician waxing lyrical about my rivetingly exciting fishing hobby. But then I ask myself, since publishers seem to require the participation of a literary agent - surely if literary agents were expert, successful, accomplished writers, they would be writing books? Are they experts in anything, or do they just bring people with a public profile already formed, to the top of a strategically placed table top at the front of a Waterstones branch? Do they even have a mandate to, or interest in, taking chances and risks, or seeking out edgy and brave content? It seems that the daughter of a sister of a neighbour of an actor that appeared in a soap opera for three weeks in 1986, has a new diet and gym regime book out - one can only imagine the stampede to get hold of that.

Yes, I'll probably be waiting a long, long time if I don't just take it into my own hands, and accept that only half a dozen people might ever hear of my efforts, and that the book's 'merit' will be measured and quantified by random judgements by the random opinions of some 'random phantoms'.

But I have not been idle. I have been shown interest and support by some great people that have told me they are keen to read what I have written. I have two personal Facebook accounts with a (steadily growing) aggregate of over 7,000 friends. A 'writer' page with almost 1,800 followers. A 'book' page with almost 500.

An anti-Brexit Facebook group with over 700 members. My new ventures into the worlds of Twitter and Instagram have fledgling status. Each of these social media presences has been accumulated at the same time as I have been writing and editing this work, over less than six months, and I will communicate in that sphere and grow those numbers as best I can. When it comes right down to the bottom line, and I am not meaning a 'bottom line' in the capitalist's bible (i.e. the profit margin), this book has only had to satisfy one person which is myself.

Only the writer, or the artist, or the musician, or the poet, has to believe in their creations in order for the existence of those creations to be justified. So, this book exists.

Stuart Watkins, Yorkshire, June 2019.

Abortion

'Abortion', definition: 'termination'.
This piece is about the most common use of the word.

"The opinion of even the most insightful man on the subject of abortion is barely valid, because it is based on the complete absence of the relevant experience, biology, and, therefore, understanding of the matter. It carries no weight." - Me.

....

Abortion.
Tricky issue? Not really.
Moral dilemma? Not really.
Discussion topic laden with morality?
Absolutely.
But dilemma? Not necessarily.
That depends on which - and whose -
situation is being looked at, and by whom.

I am a man – which
has profound relevance to this topic,
especially because of the words
and the 'trains of logical thought'
I am going to address it with.

There are a few relevant facts to outline
before I even begin my commentary:

1) As a man, I cannot conceive a new human being within my body, although I can impregnate a woman so that she carries a new human being.

9

2) I therefore have neither the experience, nor the knowledge, that a woman, that has, or has had, a new human being begin its life within her body, possesses.

3) My body has a hormone called testosterone, that forms a large part of my masculinity, bubbling around within it.

4) Women have two hormones, oestrogen and progesterone, that form a large part of their femininity, within the bodies that they inhabit.

These facts are going to form some of the logical thought processes that I wish to use in the exploration of the subject.

As a citizen of the so-called United Kingdom, where we are permitted to speak freely, I am, as an adult male of arguably sound mind, entitled to an opinion on general matters like this. But my opinion on this particular subject cannot carry the same level of understanding as that of a woman that has, or has had, a new human being growing within her body, and our opinions on this, hers and mine, are affected not just from this deeply different level of actual experience, but also from our profoundly different physiology.

Our body parts of course, and, crucially, those different hormones.

Please forgive me, if you'll pardon the childish pun, that I am addressing the trains of relevant, logical thought through what are often termed 'baby steps'.

I see this as essential, first so that I do not lose people of limited logical capability, and also because I am viewing the topic from angles that are not necessarily in line with the 'normal' narratives of the debate.

So, I am entitled to an opinion, I am entitled to contribute to the debate, but only from the vastly inferior perspective of a male, while a female, whether she has first-hand experience of carrying a new human being or not, since the very capability of conceiving, and the differing hormones, make a critical and profound difference to our levels of understanding. All of this childish, baby step logic (about children and babies as it happens) is necessary to prepare the ground for the extrapolation of logic and the lateral thinking, (or as some say 'out of the box'), that I am about to start to discuss.

So, we have sufficient foundations
to make some declarations:

1) Men can have no experience or understanding of what it is like to conceive and carry a foetus, an embryo, a child, a brand new human being.
2) We extend the line of that logic to a crucial level, to reach the point I wish to make as the primary reason that this piece of writing exists.
3) I believe, and assert, that in any vote or decision-making process of any kind men should play no part, as we are wholly unqualified. Our opinions should be voiced, considered and taken into account, but our participation must logically end at that point.

4)   The power of the actual decision should rest 100% with women. Not even 99%. 100%.

That is the basic theory.

There is now the matter of practical specifics.

Man impregnates woman.
Was it a mutual act, or was it rape?
If it had been a mutual act,
there are a spectrum of possibilities
such as:
Are they a couple conceiving intentionally?
And if the answer to that is yes,
abortion is highly unlikely to figure!
If the answer is no, an accidental conception,
let's assume the mother and father discuss their
options, and their feelings,
and make a mutual decision about their choice.
In this case an agreed abortion is a possible
outcome.
Keeping the child is also a possible agreement,
and then abortion is again irrelevant.

But now let's suppose they disagree.

Suppose the man wants to keep the child
but the woman wants an abortion,
or vice versa.
Either way - either way,
the conceived human being is alive
within the body of the woman,
and so whilst the man's view can be heard,
the final decision - either way,

must be taken by the woman.
In not just my opinion,
but also by irrefutable, absolute, logic.

Now let us consider a conception by rape.
I feel that it is almost unthinkable
that I should even have to dissect this at all.
By any measure of morality,
by any measure of humanity,
and even with the primitive understanding
that a man could possess of such a scenario,
normal empathy,
normal humanity,
normal morality,
and normal basic respect,
says that one can imagine,
maybe even to the limited, theoretical extent
that a man could even begin to grasp,
an abortion would be the only option
for many women.
The opposing view, keeping the child,
though there have been many such examples
where women have elected to do so,
surely can only be her choice alone.
Fully supported and accommodated
by all branches of society
and its entire legal framework.

Nothing else is logical,
nothing else is moral.

Unfortunately the Catholic Church,
full of wholly unqualified male officials,
many with questionable mindsets
as is fortunately common knowledge,

would have me in the wrong on the matter.
Logic and religion by definition do not co-exist.

Jacob Rees-Mogg,
you may have heard of him.
Old-fashioned term 'toff'.
Educated at all-male Eton College,
which you may have heard of.
He followed that with Trinity College, Oxford.
Which again, you may know of.
He studied history .... ah, you're ahead of me.
Not mathematics,
nor a science.
The razor-sharp and profoundly logical mind
of a student of history.
I wish to retain the baby steps of perspective
and not lose anybody,
especially the history graduates among us.

Mr. Rees-Mogg
is very fond of preaching to people,
he does it every single day, because it's his day job.
He endeavours to convey the impression
that he has a command of common sense,
and the ability to think logically.

Impressionable Brexit supporters flock to his
silver-spoon accent
and economic analysis,
as if the domestic economics of
a multi-millionaire,
reportedly to the tune of £100,000,000,
relate in any way to the average family.
But he's jovial,
condescending, patronising,

rude, in a cheeky, humorous way,
as if the whole thing is just
a friendly game of verbal tennis.
In other words, frivolous point-scoring.
A smug, self-appointed expert.
Can the British electorate,
even the most racist,
Right-Wing-Press reading,
easy-to-convince Brexiteers,
honestly not spot the fact that
he cannot possibly understand
the lives of most of us,
we average people, that have only a
net worth of, say,
£50,000,000?
Or maybe a net worth of zero,
living from pay-cheque to pay-cheque,
juggling credit card balances,
without equity in our homes,
or in our rented homes,
with perhaps an out-of-control
and unauthorised overdraft?

Are people honestly,
seriously, convinced by such a posh,
patronising, pompous, self-important twerp,
made from, it seems, the exact same mould as
Boris Johnson and Nigel Farage?

They are people who look and talk down
to everybody they speak to.
I politely suggest there may be a
need for some people to
wake the fuck up.

As for the self-appointed experts,
my observation,
my assessment,
my opinion,
based on many years of studious judgement,
is that very, very rarely
is a politician any kind of expert.

However, they do always have plenty of
nothing to say.

I would like to lob some of my own logical thoughts
into the mix.

I mentioned the Catholic Church.

Jacob Rees-Mogg is a Catholic,
and guess (the Hell) what?
Jacob's logic,
as a devout Catholic,
that church full of and run by men,
is as follows.

The conception of a human being is when
Spermatozoa and Ovum connect.
Day 1.
Conception day.
Crucially that occurs,
unless a test tube is involved,
inside the body of a woman.
I remind you that Jacob is not a woman,
and is of course completely clueless of
how she might, or could, possibly feel.

His attempts to pass a comment of any relevance

are akin to a tortoise trying to give
a flying lesson to an eagle.

His unqualified opinion is that
if that woman has been raped,
she should not be allowed to abort the pregnancy.

Unbelievably,
there are people that want him as Prime Minister.
No doubt he is popular amongst
wife-beaters and 'men' that abuse their daughters,
'men' that have no respect for women,
there are plenty of them about.
Ask the police.
The male officials of the Catholic Church
do not marry.
They do not raise families.
They are, in theory, celibate,
which means not to indulge in sexual activity.
As we all now know, that rule gets widely broken
in the most awful of ways.

Jacob Rees-Mogg
seems very much in his element
when telling others what to do
and looking down on them.
I concede that that is only my opinion.
Other opinions are available.

This is a supposedly clever man,
that believes in,
on the one hand,
an invisible man in the sky.
(He's definitely not a woman, this invisible man.)
On the other hand, Jacob thinks

17

that he has some capacity for logic.
Can you spot the tiny contradiction?

Mr. Rees-Mogg is not usually the kind of man
that holds back on what he thinks,
yet though he is a parent of six children,
I have not heard him speak once
in those charming, supercilious, pompous tones
about the elephant in the room,
the matter of priests
and children in the Catholic Church.

After all, it's certainly no longer secret material.
What are your views, Mr. Rees-Mogg?
Please train your mastery of advanced logic,
your eloquence,
your precision microscope of a historian's genius,
on that subject, if you would be so kind.
What do you feel the Church should do about it?
Offer up some intellectual advice,
it's your speciality after all. Help them out.

This is exactly the kind of man, and men,
that should be nowhere near decisions about
abortions.
Up to, and even, and in fact especially, the Pope.

I have a little snippet of advice for all men,
including myself,
since I have been imparting
my excuse for wisdom on this page.

I suggest that we
give our opinions,
exercise our right to free speech,

and then shut our big, stupid mouths
and let the women,
who know what the issues are,
and the emotions are,
and are the only ones
actually equipped to discuss them
and decide upon them meaningfully,
make their decisions
without our unqualified,
busybody interference.

This is not only logically, and biologically,
outside the domain of men;
it is morally outside the domain of men.

I should not have had to write a single word of that.

Child of The World

I was born in a part of India,
I am a Hindu.
I was born in a different part of India,
I am a Muslim.
I was born in another part of India,
I am a Sikh.
I was born in Italy,
I am a Catholic.
I was born in Saudi Arabia,
I am a Muslim.
I was born in Israel,
I am a Jew.
I was born in the United States of America,
I am a Christian, a Baptist.
I was born in a particular part of the USA,
I am a Mormon.
I was born of the Earth,
I am a Pagan, a Druid.
I was born in Russia,
I was raised within the Russian Orthodox Church.
I was born in Greece
and raised within the Greek Orthodox Church.
I was born in no particular location,
I am a Jehovah's Witness.
I was born in any random area of the world,
I worship Money.

My parents, my schoolteachers and my elders
assure me that everything I am told
is the absolute truth.

All of it, fact.

It is all other belief structures that are wrong.
Ours is the only true path.
It is not appropriate to think
that what I have been taught,
and instructed and expected to believe,
is dependent only on geography,
and circumstance,
and therefore arbitrary and random?

....

It is not appropriate for me to ask questions.
It is not appropriate to doubt
the veracity of what I have been told.

It is not appropriate to have an open mind.

It is not appropriate to ask;
"If our way is the truth,
why are there all these other faiths?
Why doesn't everybody follow
the same path if it is the truth?
I don't understand."

It is not appropriate to ask;
"Why do we cut off the hand of a thief,
stone a woman to death,
or behead someone for
atheism, blasphemy,
or for being homosexual?
I don't understand."

It is not appropriate to ask;
"Why was my penis mutilated
as a baby?
I don't understand."

It is not appropriate to ask;
"How can bread and wine possibly be
the actual flesh and blood of a man?
I don't understand."

It is not appropriate to ask;
"Why must I die
rather than be given a transfusion of blood?
I don't understand."

It is not appropriate
to suggest that all religions
are just man-made constructs.

It is not appropriate to point out
that the multiple gods
of Greece, Rome, Egypt and Scandinavia
were believed in no less
than today's creeds and doctrines.
Yet nobody believes in those any more,
and have not for many, many years.
If I did, I'd be ridiculed and mocked.
"Surely that will be the eventual fate
of all that I have been told?
Forgotten, lost, like the visage and memory
of Ozymandias?"

Long ago,
before the advancement
and development of science,
I expect that I too
would have found great difficulty in comprehending:

The Sun and the Moon,
Thunder and Lightning,

Good and Evil.
The Night Sky, the Stars.
The myriad and variety of species of animals.
The flight of birds.
The origins of mankind.

It would, I expect, seem to me a very believable
explanation
that a host of deities,
with specific responsibilities,
would be making all of that happen.
No more or less credible, instead,
a single omnipotent and omnipresent deity
(who always, curiously, seems to be male,
in spite of the fact that
the creator and nurturer
of life and love
within nature
is generally female),
carrying out all the functions of the many gods.

But over the years, just look at the revelations of
science,
not to be confused with the biblical Book of
Revelation
and its account of Armageddon.

Scientists investigated, discovered and explained
many things, a few of them being:

Celestial bodies - planets, comets, stars,
quasars, pulsars, asteroids,
supernovae, black holes.
The speed of light.
The speed of sound.

23

Weather systems - tornadoes, hurricanes, typhoons,
lightning, thunder.
The electromagnetic spectrum -
coloured light, the rainbow of red to violet,
the infra-red, the ultraviolet,
X-rays, Gamma rays, microwaves, radio waves.
Gravitational forces. Relativity.
The space-time continuum.
Atoms, molecules, protons, electrons,
neutrons, quarks, neutrinos.
Electricity.
Thermodynamics.
Magnetism.
Momentum.
Quantum mechanics.
Mammals, molluscs, amphibians, reptiles, rodents,
insects, arachnids, crustaceans, fish.
The structures and behaviour of living cells.
Gases, liquids, solids, emulsions, gels, aerosols.
Chemical elements, chemical compounds.
Acids, alkalis.
Metals, non-metals.
Advances in medicine and anatomy.
Pharmacology, pharmaceuticals.
Friction. Propulsion.
Astrophysics and astronomy.
Nuclear fission, nuclear fusion.
Fossils, dinosaurs, geology, palaeontology,
the determination of the age of the Earth.

And, of course, the big one, evolution.
Inventors gave us cars, aeroplanes, hot air balloons,
ocean liners, submarines and helicopters.
Satellites, rockets to the moon.
Unmanned space explorer craft.

Telephones, televisions, computers, household
appliances. Skyscrapers, bridges, tunnels.
Guns, bombs, missiles, explosives, vehicles of war.

Yet it is still, for some, not appropriate to apply any
logic.
All the explanations that science has revealed
are insufficient, they are not enough.

It is not appropriate to consider verifiable facts.

(Blind) Faith is therefore necessary,
as there are no facts to call upon.

Even Epicurus, who died long ago, in 270 BC, applied
acute and irrefutable logic to the idea of God, thus:

"Is God willing to prevent evil, but not able?
Then He is not omnipotent.
Is He able, but not willing?
Then He is malevolent.
Is He both able, and willing?
Then whence cometh evil?
Is He neither able nor willing?
Then why call Him God?"

Is there any difference between a cult and a religion
other than the number of people that follow it?
Who decides what that number is?
What is that number?
Is it a fluke that the word 'culture'
contains the word 'cult'?

The Democratic Will of The People
(Brexit Pt. 1)

On the 26th June 2016,
there was a referendum to establish
the Will Of The People
of the so-called United Kingdom
with regard to either
Remain in the European Union
or
Leave the European Union.

Much to the glee of xenophobes and true patriots
the length and breadth of our
so-called United Kingdom,
the result was apparently an emphatic landslide
of - to one decimal place -
51.9% to Leave over 48.1% to Remain.

Not surprisingly, those victorious folks
who had voted to
leave the European Union,
felt they had the right to use terms such as
The Will Of The People, and
The Triumph Of Democracy, and
proceeded to offer up a great many permutations of
What We Voted For, and
Brexit means Brexit, and
Walk Away, the British People have spoken!
After all, the result had been so
decisive and unambiguous.

Before exploring this a single word,
or thought, further,

26

a brace of facts are of distinct and profound
relevance;
the people of Northern Ireland voted to
Remain in the European Union, and by a margin of -
to one decimal place -
<u>55.8% to Remain over 44.2% to Leave.</u>

The Will Of The Northern Irish People had spoken.

The people of Scotland also voted to
Remain in the European Union, and by a margin of -
to one decimal place -
<u>62.0% to Remain over 38% to Leave.</u>

The Will of The Scottish People had spoken.

….…

I am aware that not all people have the same grasp
of mathematics, or even rudimentary arithmetic.

Therefore, to try and make things simple
before exploring the matter further still,
let me clarify the figures, in the hope of keeping
calculations at the simplest possible level,
so that everything is as clear as a bell.

The figures for this so-called United Kingdom,
sometimes called the Precious Union, were

Britain overall: <u>51.9% to Leave.</u>
Northern Ireland overall: <u>55.8% to Remain.</u>
Scotland overall: <u>62.0% to Remain.</u>

Of course the most important principle
which is said to be applied in this entire matter

is the matter of
Democracy!
The Will of The People!
This is stated very clearly as sacred,
by supporters of the overall vote,
but they do not seem to understand the principle..

At least, beyond that
superficial,
one-dimensional perception.

Yet since, by their own assertion, their own belief,
the expressed view of the majority of voters is to be
honoured
over and above the expressed view of the minority of
voters,
I see it as necessary to apply some logical extensions.

The tale of Ireland.
For a long time there were Troubles there.
Old differences.
The Republic in the South,
the allegiances to Westminster in the North.
The North felt a pride in being a part of the
so-called United Kingdom.
They believed that they were respected, and
protected,
by the administration in London.
Many were killed and injured in the Troubles,
perpetrated by both sides,
suffered by both sides.
Violence was propagated for a long time,
it was felt by many to be an insoluble issue
though most people had dreams of peace.
After a peace process lasting a number of years,

in the year of 1998,
the Good Friday Agreement was signed,
which delivered, and maintained,
peace since that day,
and the 'rigorous impartiality' that
the British Government
pledged and committed to observe and apply,
held fast until the shame of its abuse
after the General Election of 2017.

A certain Mrs. Theresa May,
esteemed Prime Minister of Britain,
in order to continue to be able to
discharge her duties,
decided that her own self-interest
was more important than honouring that agreement,
and that rigorous impartiality was covered
in the urine and faeces
of contempt, disrespect and irresponsibility.
She decided to use taxpayers' money
for personal motives.
She had said that there was no such thing as a
Magic Money Tree
yet she shook its branches, for it did exist after all,
and in setting fire to the Good Friday Agreement,
a billion-plus English taxpayers' pounds
were offered as a bribe
to buy her the…….10……DUP votes in Parliament
that enabled her to keep her job.
Public money, that was not available for
the NHS, or the police,
suddenly, magically,
appeared for her to splash around
as if it were from her own personal savings.
Utter contempt for both

the spirit
and the letter
of an agreement
that had achieved something that
many never felt possible,
treated as if it were nothing. Except, perhaps,
toilet paper.
How is that even within the law?
Billion pound bribes?
The buying of votes with public money?
By what mad definition of corruption is that <u>not</u>
corruption?

One can be sure that if Jeremy Corbyn were to do
such a thing,
the media would adorn the robes of judge, jury and
executioner
and he'd be drummed unceremoniously from power,
or at least the
machines of Propaganda
would do their utmost
to achieve that outcome.
Mr. Corbyn had ironically been accused, by Mrs. May,
that if he were to become Prime Minister
he would be irresponsible with public money......

And where were the newspapers, or the BBC,
or any other media outlet,
that are supposed to be there
to hold criminals to account?

Where was the outrage,
the witch hunt?
Was it not a dishonest act?
And so back to the pressing matter of the Holy Brexit.

During the referendum campaigns,
that were full of lies and misinformation,
we heard not a peep about Ireland.
How on Earth could anybody even think that with the
Republic Of Ireland in the South
remaining in the European Union,
and the North being steamrollered out of the EU,
against their will,
even though they had voted Remain
by a bigger margin than the
so-called United Kingdom had voted Leave,
frog-marched out at the will of
English and Welsh voters,
could possibly be anything other
than a huge constitutional issue
and an almighty operational mess?
Part of Ireland remaining in the EU,
part of Ireland leaving the EU.
Not given even the slightest attention in
the run-up to the referendum.
Oversight, deliberate omission,
too complicated, confusing?
Take your pick of reasons. All of the above?
The Will Of The People, all of a sudden,
not seemingly as relevant.
Whatever the Brexit Deal (Or No Deal) looks like,
we can hardly be surprised
if an independence referendum takes place
up there in Northern Ireland.
We can hardly be surprised
if a vote for independence is decided on,
and by a landslide.
We can hardly be surprised
if as soon as that independence occurs,
Northern Ireland don't sign themselves

straight back into the European Union
that they never wanted to leave in the first place.
We can hardly be surprised
if now that Northern Ireland can be
absolutely certain
that their faith in Westminster is unjustified,
that their faith in Westminster is a mistake,
then a United Ireland, a Republic with proud
restored membership of the European Union,
may simply be a formality, a foregone conclusion.

'United Kingdom'? 'Precious Union'?

No. The Will Of Your People is worthless.
You will do as you are directed by the
Will Of Other People.
Democracy, apparently,
just selectively applied.

—·—

It doesn't look anything like a united kingdom to me,
since individual nations of the precious union
are disregarded and treated like
second-class citizens.
A 51.9% to 48.1% scrape of a majority for the
whole of Britain
is virtually a split straight down the middle,
which is not unity either.

That pathetic excuse for a decision being used
to drum a nation that wants to stay in the EU, out of it.

The Will of The People is paramount?
It seems that the will of some people
is more paramount than that of others.

Democracy is sacrosanct, sometimes.
It depends who you are,
and who it benefits and suits.
Some of the people that it suits wear suits.

The tale of Scotland.
Almost 2000 years ago it was
that the Roman Emperor Hadrian built a wall
to separate the occupied England
from the unoccupied Scotland.
Perhaps I am going back a tad far,
but the fact that the
mighty and legendary Roman Empire,
some 1,671 million square miles in area,
decided to section off Scotland
by building Hadrian's Wall,
73 miles in length,
rather than invade it,
is an interesting fact to say the very least.
The Scots have always been a proud bunch.
Their victory at the Battle of Stirling Bridge in 1297.
William Wallace executed for treason
for opposing the English.
Their victory at the Battle of Bannockburn in 1314.
The great Robert the Bruce that led
the independent Scots.

Much later, classic skirmishes at
Murrayfield, Ibrox and Hampden,
Scots often revelling in defeating the English
with somewhat less violence and bloodshed,
though blood has certainly been spilt
at Murrayfield now and then.

That fact reminds me of a famous saying;
"football is a game where
men pretend to be injured,
rugby is a game where they pretend not to be."

For a substantial proportion of the so-called United Kingdom, leaving the European Union is regarded as possibly the biggest mistake of our lifetime, and we may soon find out whether it was though that is still avoidable. The referendum foolishly empowered the least intelligent Britons with the same value of vote as the most intelligent Britons, and I will refer to this again. Racism against minorities, immigrants, other EU states and the EU itself has spiked in the ugliest of social landscapes in recent memory. The online chatrooms reek of it every single day.

The Depths of The Subconscious

Ah! What was that!
I awaken, startled, there must have been a noise.
The slam of a car door,
the low, gruff bark of a substantial dog,
maybe even the shriek of an angry cat.
Perhaps a bang from my neighbours' side of the wall.

I glance at the clock at my bedside
in the pitch blackness,
at the red LED image,
it's 3.12am.

No sooner is my head resting again on the soft pillow
than I am drifting away as if I had
never awakened at all.

I am in a house. It's tall. It seems to have a number of
floors and a great many rooms, maybe twenty or
more rooms, maybe five or six storeys high if one
includes the cellar. I feel younger, I know where I am
and I know when it is.
This is Oxford in mid-December, I am at university.
It's as if it were yesterday, as if it were today,
as if it were right here, and right now.

The house is full of party, I smell the unmistakable
cannabis and the tobacco, the cheap wine
and there is more than a trace of vomit
in this particular room as well.
Someone has misjudged
their capacity to abuse their body.
The sweat, and the resulting stench

35

of collective body odour,
of the sheer volume of unwashed students
that seem to occupy
every tiny space and corner
of every room.
It's a miasma of decadence and stupor.

But where is my girlfriend, Michelle?

I know we arrived here together, it's a party though,
and so I need to explore the place
to find out which room of the 'twenty or more' she has
wandered into.

As I weave in and out of the rooms
I overhear discussions,
giving expert analysis of Plato's Republic,
or expert analysis of Einstein's Theory Of Relativity,
or expert analysis of Da Vinci's polymathic genius,
or expert analysis of the creativity of
Frank Lloyd Wright,
or expert analysis of the work of Stephen Hawking,
or expert analysis of Chaucer's Canterbury Tales.

Perhaps the exhaustive inspired works of
Shakespeare
or the macabre darkness of
Dante's Inferno,
or of Poe or Lovecraft.
Expert analysis of the slaughter of Native Americans,
or the expert analysis of the
unworkability of communism
or the expert analysis of the
unworkability of capitalism.

(Most people should know that neither of them work,
that they result in virtually identical outcomes,
just by different routes).

Opinions from the
Red Clowns to the Left of me
and the Blue Jokers to the Right,
and me stuck in the middle.

Intellectual critiques of the art
of Van Gogh, Picasso and Rembrandt,
Dali, Magritte, and 'Banksy''s audacious sabotage
of his own work at auction.
The aesthetic splendour of the creations of
Barbara Hepworth or Paul Klee.

Expert explanations of the properties
of all the chemical
elements of the Periodic Table,
the ins and outs of quantum mechanics,
thermodynamics
and superstring theory,
or, say, the expert analysis of atheism versus
any other belief system or religion.
Meticulous, measured analysis of the music of
Mozart, Beethoven, Liszt and Paganini,
Pink Floyd and the Spice Girls,
Miles Davis and The Beatles.
A heated debate is raging on the subject of:

'Who is the best drummer that ever lived?'
Moon? Bonham? Rich? Cobham?
Bruford? Colaiuta? Gadd? Peart? Portnoy?
What about the insights of
Galileo, Eratosthenes and Ptolemy,

or the riddle of Fermat's Last Theorem
that confounded mathematicians for 358 years?
The infinite perfection of Pi, or of
the Fibonacci Series and Golden Ratio?

There is a small huddle of ugly, shady, racist
characters discussing Brexit,
they seem to identify themselves
as the "British Bulldog's Freedom Fighters."
Across the room, within earshot,
listening and laughing,
another huddle
who have coined them a different name,
they refer to the first group as the
"Brain Dead Imbecile Club".

I move on, ears pinned back.
A couple of groups are talking about Dan Bongino,
who the hell is Dan Bongino?
Let's pop his name into our preferred
internet search engines,
see how deep the rabbit hole goes,
as Morpheus would put it...
"Was the real Russian collusion by Clinton and not
Trump at all?
Follow the money, and the uranium."
Hey, who said that?
It was a ghostly, sourceless whisper in my ear.

I'm momentarily spooked.
There are always Spooks.

Students are sometimes convinced they know
everything, while others are completely open-minded

to learn things, and hence,
such deep and broad discussions
abound and propagate.
I am both the open-minded sponge and the arrogant
know-all depending on the subject matter,
so I move from room to room
to indulge in the cosmic discourse.
In some instances I learn, and in others I teach,
and in others I both learn and teach simultaneously.

But where's Michelle?

All the rooms in the big house have numbers on them
because it is a student-house,
divided up to house the maximum number of people
and generate the maximum amount of rental income.

Perhaps four or five of the
aforementioned conversations
take place in each of the rooms.
While putting the world or academic knowledge
under the philosophical microscope,
I gradually drink enough cheap wine and cheap beer
to lose my awareness of everything around me.
I am still involved in intellectual to-ing and fro-ing,
but it is now on auto-pilot,
and so I have no clue what I am hearing or saying.

It is probably drivel;
both what I am hearing is probably drivel
and what I am saying is probably drivel
because we are all inebriated and as high as kites.
Somebody accuses me of ripping them off
in a computer game
to the tune of £20.

39

Somebody else's girlfriend accuses me
of the improper suggestion
that she and I carry out some obscene acts
in front of a webcam.
I don't even know how to use a webcam.

My memory is full of broken half-memories by now
and so I cannot remember what I said to anybody,
nor can I recall whether I even played a video game.

Again I recall that I came into the house with
Michelle, so I stand up,
at the fourth attempt after three unsuccessful ones,
and begin to explore once again.
Although, other than her, all the people in the house
are complete strangers,
with forgettable and unfamiliar faces,
the deep and intellectual discussions
of the last however long
mean that I am able to recognise people
in most of the rooms.
I will have told them my name
and they will have told me theirs,
yet I will not be able to remember any of those
identifiers, just like I cannot remember a single word
of the content
of anything we have talked about.
I decide to be systematic -
and search for Michelle from the cellar to the attic -
which should be less problematic -
and almost automatic,
especially since most of my
senses are severely impaired
due to the various substances in my blood.

I find her in the room with the number 13 on the door,
which for a few brief moments
plays havoc with my triskaidekaphobia,
but it passes quickly,
as I am too disengaged for coherent thought.
I sit with her.
She's in a similar state of mind.
So rather than attempt anything cerebral,
we giggle, talk gibberish,
and choose not to move for a while.

However.

You know how it is when you can sense
imminent rain?
The humidity, colour of the sky,
the moisture on the air?
The subtle changes in
the sensation of the surroundings?
Well.
As we sit there on the floor of room 13,
and it does not make any sense to
try to blame the number on the door,
but in the way one senses that impending rainfall,
I was able to detect an
ominous darkness and evil
at that moment.

In looking around me,
nothing physical had changed whatsoever.

Those endless unfamiliar faces.
Their conversations uninterrupted,
their number no greater or fewer,
their countenance oblivious to

41

the marauding presence.
There is something else about
the approaching danger.
Frequencies and vibrations, at levels that my heart
is able to decipher, sense, interpret and understand.
The specific aim of the 'presence' is to
cut out my heart –
but it is my heart
that senses the motive of the threat,
even though the danger has,
at least at this point,
no physical manifestation or form.

….…

Michelle and I help each other to our feet
and leave the house.
We step out into the extreme winter cold
and then, all of a sudden,
I am somewhere completely different.

Michelle has vanished.

I am tied to a metal pole,
with my hands fastened behind my back
and around the pole.
The pole is atop a hill, 50 or 60 metres high,
rising above a level plain.
There is an identical hill, of a similar height,
some 80 metres to my left,
and my childhood best friend
is similarly bound to a metal pole at its summit.
There is a large gathering of spectators
around the two hills, and, respectfully,
nobody stands on the slopes of the grassy domes.

A lightning storm is about to be unleashed
and the poles will shortly receive the bolts.

It is a double execution by forces of nature,
and the crowd's anticipation is at fever pitch.

I close my eyes, and wait for
the instantaneous boiling of my blood.

At the moment of incineration,
as if being immediately transported
to a new astral plane
and sphere of consciousness
in a split-second,
I feel my body, mind and spirit
explode in excruciating white heat,
and I awaken somewhere new.

I am moving.

The scenario is closest to,
although not all that close to,
the sensation of being in a car
at a point on a motorway,
in the dark, on approaching a nameless city,
where there are bright, orange sodium lights
flashing past every nano-second.

Suddenly the passing lights have disappeared
as quickly as they materialised.

I am back at the house, but alone, 'sans-Michelle',
as if she were an island at high tide.

Although the darkness and its portentous tangibility

43

have disappeared,
I am equally afraid because I am being pursued
by a different entity entirely,
and am still in grave danger.

The cheap wine and the cheap beer within me
cause me to need to use the bathroom,
even though the bathroom,
like every other room,
is full of people,
so I just have to urinate in front of everybody.
It would be pointless to ask them to move
as they are at least as drunk
and incapacitated as I am.
Even though they aren't interested in looking
it still feels a little strange,
and therefore I have to use extra concentration
and extra relaxation
at the same time
to accomplish the task, which I succeed in doing.

In what seems like about another 10 minutes or so,
that all-encompassing darkness and my fear of it
return as acutely as before.
I decide that the simplest way to escape is to run,
so I run,
but I notice that I am running
down unfamiliar roads in an
unfamiliar place, town, city.
I turn left, and right, and right, and left,
but I cannot lose the source of my fright.

It is not gaining ground,
but it is not losing ground either,
so I have to maintain my speed,

44

but I am unable to break away
because I have insufficient energy
with which to accelerate.
At this point I remember
that I possess the ability to fly,
and so I take off from the ground
as if I have grabbed the guide-rope
of a hot air balloon.
My ascent, for a time, vertical, and rapid.

When I reach a certain height
I adjust and fly horizontally,
and I am free,
away from the doom of 'whatever it was'.

I fly for 100 miles or so,
and then I bring myself back to Earth
in an English city,
but I do not recognise anything about it.
The streets look like those in an English city
such as - say -
London, or Bristol, or Manchester, or Birmingham,
but I have been to all of those
and would recognise
a road, or a street, or a landmark,
but there is nothing.
Where did I park my car?
Which of the various cars
that I have owned over the years
am I trying to find?
Which make and model?
What colour?
What is the registration number?
I am in my past now,
but at which part of my past?

Where is this place?
Residential roads,
such as those in any borough of London.

Brent Cross?
Notting Hill?
Lewisham?
Greenwich?

Lines of houses,
and lines of cars parked outside them.
What is the name of the street where I parked?
Am I looking for my Volkswagen?
My Alfa Romeo? Sapphire, my beloved blue BMW?
My memory is an actual sieve, and of no use.

—·—

I am aware now that I am in a dream,
perhaps for the first time
since that 'noise' briefly woke me.
My mind is half-conscious and half in full sleep
which means that I can control
this predicament a little,
with the tiny amount of actual consciousness I have.
I do not recognise the city
and I do not remember the date,
I cannot remember the car or its registration number
and I am therefore irretrievably lost.
The conscious element of my thoughts
begins to recede.
I then notice that as well as my having no recognition
of the place, to add insult to injury
I am trapped.
There are dead-ends everywhere.
The collection of roads and streets

46

is actually an elaborate maze.
I cannot find any way out and now,
the impending darkness and evil
is back on my tail.

Then I see that I actually have a tail myself, a real tail.
I wonder whether I am not human,
but some other animal,
then I realise that I am a human being that has a tail.
Whereabouts will the spaceship be landing?
I cannot see any trace of the extraterrestrial visitors,
yet the confusion of telepathic murmurs
are coming through -
can I find them before the atmosphere of the
pursuing force envelops me?

I think I will be caught
before I know where the aliens are.
I am still confined within the frustration of the maze,
and still being chased by the cloud of malevolence.

There is only one solution to this Nightmare,
and that is
to do what I have, over the years, learned to do.

I will summon and connect my conscious mind
to wake myself up.

So, the technique is;
Within the Nightmare,
I lay on the ground and relax every muscle.
Within the Nightmare,
I close my eyes.
I can then, somehow, but it always works,
Within the Nightmare

47

I imagine myself dreaming, in my bed.
I focus, concentrate, and then connect.

Somehow my consciousness is able to move
from the subconscious to the conscious.
Instead of being on the ground within the Nightmare,
I am in my bed, and I wake.

Sometimes it is a 'clean wake',
and at other times,
the Nightmare fights me,
and a battle takes place
where I 'half-wake'
but then am sucked back into the Nightmare.

The battle continues,
until I win it.
That's how you win battles;
not to be the one that stops fighting.
And so I do always win that battle.

It is simply a question of how many times
I have to repeat the cycle of 'half-waking'.

And so,
the Nightmare is over,
and I am awake.

I look across at the LED numbers beside me.

It's 3.15am.

The Great British Fallacy

(and its shameful, shameless, underlying deceit)

"The monarchy brings in more money, through the tourist income it attracts, than it costs to the taxpayer".

We have all heard this statement, it seems, hundreds of times.

It is trotted out, parrot-fashion, by supporters of the monarchy in all and any debates, to justify the very existence of the Royal Family.

To suggest that they are 'good value for money'.

To also suggest that the opposing view, that they are parasites leeching off the British people, is <u>FACTUALLY</u> untrue.

I see no interviewer or debater properly questioning it, no holding the claimant to account for making the declaration, and no demand for proof.

Such a bold claim, that they are, factually, financially beneficial to the country, that needs proof - and since it is only a matter of numbers and calculations, what is the problem in proving it to everybody?

Well, I have never seen anybody prove it, I have never seen anybody try to prove it, and I have never seen anybody demand that a claimant prove it.

What is this recurring theme of weak, ineffective questioning, by interviewers that are supposed to be professionals at doing it?

You would imagine a huge salary would require a decent set of skills would you not, I think it's a criticism that one could level fairly at the so-called professionals.

So the words, the empty claims, are left unchallenged every single time they are said, they get repeated time after time after time after time, by different royalists with no grounding in science or mathematics - repetition is a well-versed technique of Propaganda, that causes it to be believed in the absence of scrutiny, in this case to give the monarchy an implied, but only implied, legitimacy.

Whenever I see or hear this flimsy myth of a claim, the temperature of my blood reaches boiling point within seconds.

My mind spins into a maelstrom of analytical anger.

My very psyche gets sucked into a whirling tornado that wrenches me into the ionosphere with the sheer, raw frustration of the unchallenged lie, and yet another person off the hook for perpetuating a non-fact as a fact, and getting away with it.

It is time this got picked apart.

Why has nobody pulled this tissue (-paper thin) of lies, unceremoniously, to shreds yet?

It is absolute nonsense, and I will now proceed to do the necessary analysis to show that it is nonsense, so that never again will anyone be able to say it with the slightest crumb of credibility.

Let's start from the magnanimous, hypothetical assumption that it is actually true.

---·---

If it were true, the cost of the monarchy, and its copious layers of employees, and its huge expense outlay, as well as the Civil List and all of its secret, invisible, freeloading limbs of the Royal Family tree, is paid directly by the taxpayer.

But the tourist income, if we play along – just for now – that it is a larger amount of money, does not go back from whence it came, to the taxpayer, at all.

To give the mythical con-trick the tiniest chance of being true, acourate and have any validity, the money would have to be provided directly by the taxpayer and then returned directly to the taxpayer, because that is the unequivocal implication.

Tourist revenues in fact go, instead, to businesses:

Airlines.

Hotels.

Restaurants.

Petrol Stations.

Rail Companies.

Taxis.

Coach Companies.

Coffee Shops.

Shops generally.

Pubs.

Entrance fees to Museums.

Entrance fees to Ancient Sites and Monuments.

Components of our infrastructure.

So the mythical claim is already debunked, the implication and entire argument are a dishonest sham.

And so because the money does not return to the taxpayers who paid it, it is a further, specific, tax.

People are paying for the monarchy directly through their taxes, but the so-called returns are paid to completely different people, business people including, in a lot of cases, large companies and multinational corporations, without permission, or even awareness, of the taxpaying people of, in alphabetical order to eliminate favouritism, England, Northern Ireland, Scotland and Wales, the so-called United Kingdom of faithful, devoted, loyal subjects of the Crown - such as myself.

That adds an interesting touch of highly relevant perspective, does it not.

The claim is never qualified in this manner, leaving the British public with the false and deceitful impression that the outlay and the income have a direct and simple reciprocal relationship, when they absolutely do not.

People don't seem to mind, but then they are not told the whole truth, their taxes going in fact to Starbucks, Costa or McDonald's.

Perhaps they would feel somewhat differently when in possession of these additional facts.

They might be far less happy knowing that their money just ends up in the coffers, profits and the pockets of the shareholders of small, but also huge, companies.

Maybe somebody should inform them (oh, I have), and then we could find out what they actually think of this additional, sneaky, stealthy, hidden tax.

Therefore it is proven to be a falsehood, a lie, a completely over-simplistic presentation of a model that doesn't even apply, or exist, in the stated, or at least implied without any clarification, form.

You would need a highly complex set of calculations to stand the merest chance of getting any accuracy whatsoever, regarding the quantities of money that are dissipated between all those sectors, and I suggest it is completely impossible unless wild assumptions, that would greatly distort all the numbers, are utilised, which I will expand on.

This is all, by cynical design, put into a context to mislead people, and suggest the monarchy more than pays for itself - and I in this case was being extremely generous and kind, and starting from an assumption that tourist income IS greater than the cost of the monarchy, which nobody knows either way to be true or false.

I have not nearly finished, actually I have barely begun.

A question: why is it, that when some unscientific, and 'ignorant-of-advanced-thought processes' royalist tries to get away with using this imaginary claim, there are never any accompanying numbers or specific facts to prove it?

No calculations, of any form?

The answer: as they are not mathematicians, scientists, 'capable-of-advanced-thought processes', and therefore are not able to conduct an objective analysis; they do not have the knowledge or the skills to do so and then present as evidence of their assertion.

But I do, and will further illustrate the real impossibility of the lie in full detail.

A further question: why, when one of these brazen charlatans makes the spurious claim in an interview, are the numbers, the calculation, the proof, not asked for and pushed for, insisted upon, by the superficial (poor excuses for) interviewers?

The answer: because either the interviewer is incompetent, or his or her editor, and/or their producer, has been instructed to leave it as an empty, hollow statement in the hope that the wool is fully over the eyes of the poor consumers.

That the consumers would exercise their trademark gullibility and believe the words at face value, as the media always have to hope will happen - it often does.

I can, and will, pick apart the issue, and I can show why producing a meaningful calculation, to show whether the claim is indeed true or indeed untrue, is just not possible.

So, let me be clear, and let me, by contrast, be fair, honest and transparent.

I am <u>not</u> saying that I can establish that the monarchy does <u>not</u> pay for itself.

If I were to say that, it would also be a lie, and I would be showing myself to be in the same Machiavellian gutter alongside these 'Great (or Little) Deceivers'.

I <u>am</u> saying that it is an impossible calculation to do, and so anybody making a claim that the monarchy do pay for themselves, is a bare-faced liar, because they do not know, cannot know and they cannot find out.

A declaration or an assertion of it being a fact, is both factually wrong, morally wrong and deliberately misleading.

In order to either prove or disprove the assertion, we would need to isolate figures for both the full and real cost of the monarchy, and the full and real income from the tourists that come here <u>specifically</u> because of the monarchy, that are both accurate for such a calculation to be credible.

Bearing in mind that from here onwards, this is overkill, and a pointless, academic exercise of a calculation anyway, since as I have already shown, the equation is not an equation of any validity or veracity, when the income and expenditure do not even come from, and go into, the same sectors, while the implication is always that a simple, direct and reciprocal relationship exists.

I am just being thorough, approaching the matter from the relevant angles, once again so that at least somebody at last has done so.

Then, possibly, interviewers will not look so incompetent, and editors will not be so cynical, as to perpetuate the deception without rigorous, or even weak and superficial, challenges.

....

To - hypothetically - carry out an attempt to prove the frankly outrageous claim, each side - the costs and the attracted income - need to be mathematically quantified.

The easier of the two totals, the cost of the monarchy - the full cost though, and not limited to the Civil List, which is often the only amount volunteered in such discussions, that is a mere fraction of the full figure - should be comprised of, at least, these following sections of financial outlay: these are just initial thoughts off the top of my head:

1) The Civil List payouts, in their entirety, paid to every single branch and every single individual member of the extended Royal Family, without the omission of a single person or a single penny.

2) All of the salaries of every single employee, the servants, even if they are referred to differently - Buckingham Palace staff, everyone involved in the upkeep of all Crown estates i.e. the land, the buildings - every employee, and associated costs and expenses, that facilitate all travel and Royal appointments, air fares, helicopter pilots and charter fees or rentals, chauffeurs, fuel, insurance of vehicles, all security costs, incomes of permanent and temporary or contracted agents, bodyguards, employees of security services, plus of course all payments to all police officers for time spent policing Royal visits and engagements, again without the omission of a single person or penny.

3) Costs of insurance policies, that cover all of the interiors and exteriors of all royal buildings, to include every belonging, artwork, carpet, and every single artefact, including the Crown Jewels and the officials that protect them, without the omission of a single penny.

4) Decorators, cleaners, all casual or intermittent staff working or having worked in any or all capacities, without omitting a single penny.

5) Every additional penny would need to be accounted for involving any refundable expenses claimed by all members of the Civil List, and also by any Crown employee, in carrying out their roles, where they also have a facility to claim for outlays and expenses.

6) Anything else that I have not mentioned, which is spent on any matter connected to the monarchy and

its operations, no matter how small, once again to the last penny.

Clearly, in my opinion anyway, all of these monetary amounts should already be in the public domain, in full, to be looked at by anybody who wishes to, in a format that is simple to understand, since the people who pay for all of it should be able to see how and where their money is spent.

Perhaps it already is, but I doubt very much that the minute details I have listed can be viewed in one place in a comprehensive way, rather than documented and listed in lots of separate places – almost impossible to accurately quantify.

And yet we are still only on the easier half of the equation, the only half of the equation that can be measured, and even then, it is clear how difficult it is to quantify every single expense, and, in turn, the total.

One thing is certain; publicly quoted costs of maintaining the structure of the monarchy do not include the entire package, such as the rudimentary list I have offered, such as the bills for all policing of events, firstly, and then second, there would need to be transparency at a level to leave independent observers in full view of evidence of every single penny and pound spent on every single part.

I would be startled, shocked and surprised, but extremely impressed, if all of those details were happily opened up, in full, to the British people, since we pay for it.

The main reason why all the costs will not appear in full view in a single aggregated file, is precisely that it is just too complicated and fragmented to go to such lengths of so many levels of expense to collect the information, therefore I say even the easier side of the calculation cannot possibly be anything approaching accurate.

In theory though, I cannot see why any obstacle should be allowed to stand in the way of the full numbers being fully and comprehensively accessible to taxpayers, however complex the quantification of the sum, as it is surely our right to know.

Not that we could be any the wiser if secrets were kept, secrets and lies make comfortable bedfellows, and one could never accuse the British Establishment of being transparent, quite the opposite in many cases, which I will be getting to.

Before getting into the nitty-gritty of demonstrating how the relevant proportions of income from tourism cannot be quantified either, by way of interlude I have other very important points to make.

It is typical of the British, similarly to other Western countries' economic systems and their individual citizens, that this question of _financial_ justification of the monarchy, that I am showing is neither calculable nor valid as an entire argument, is seen as, it seems, the primary consideration in arguing for the justification of its existence.

As permeates capitalist systems, by definition, everything regarding feasibility comes down to money, so the fact that this issue continues to side-step such scrutiny - even when such a glaring fudge is so obviously displayed - is all the more curious, though not in the least surprising.

I say that, because I believe the most profound discussion to be had about the theory and principle of the validity of a monarchy, is not even financial at all.

The inhuman obscenity, for just one example, of Buckingham Palace containing almost 800 rooms, though I appreciate that a proportion of them are in constant or regular use, when there are hundreds of people living rough on the streets of London, within a radius of just a few miles from the Palace, is a perfect illustration of the elitist inequality in the so-called United Kingdom.

Before everyone chokes on their champagne and caviar, I am not directly advocating that hundreds of homeless people should actually be offered dwellings at the Palace, it is simply a telling indictment of the whole system, and its ridiculous and obscene values, before I go back to the arithmetical exercise.

If we assume that it is a day when the Queen is in residence at the Palace, that means that Windsor Castle, and Balmoral Castle, and Sandringham House, and goodness knows how many other properties, will be manned by the permanent employees tending to the upkeep of the properties at times when no Royal is in residence, and most of the Royals live in other private properties in any case.

The financial equation, though shown to be invalid though I shall be wielding my verbal sledgehammer a little more yet, is more of a factual comparison and attempted justification of the fortunes forked out on the monarchy, when the human argument, that monarchies are unfair, archaic, inhuman, massively unequal, have no logical reason to exist at all, and so forth, is the most valid and existential case to propose that republics are a far fairer, and better, some would say only, sociology for a 21st Century nation.

Even if tourist income could be demonstrated as being in the multi-trillions, and even if it could be demonstrated and proven that 100% of that had been brought in by the existence of the monarchy, in human terms the entire system would still, in my opinion, be an abominable abomination of abominations.

I'll now address how any attempt to find an accurate amount of tourists' money that could be attributed to the attraction of the monarchy alone is a minefield of impossibility, further showing the entire subject - much more deeply than just the unqualified lie blurted out with no evidence or accountability - has no basis in either truth or relevance.

I say relevance, as I believe and have said that in the end it comes down to whether the monarchy is itself moral or immoral, and any waste of time trying to convince people that there is something mathematically beneficial to the taxpayers, or the country, or the economy, is a distraction from that human angle, and a typical facet of the ugliness of unbridled capitalism in action.

To 'calculate' in a situation such as this, accuracy and precision are not just ideal but totally essential if such a mad, profound, outrageous claim is to hold water.

The moment that any kinds of assumptions have to enter the frame, we are approximating, and this particular example needs to employ all sorts of assumptions that will compound the inaccuracies completely off any scale.

Each assumption used compromises the results further and further.

All percentages and proportions involved in trying to carry out this calculation have to be assumed, I.e. estimated - guessed.

In order to establish, with any remote accuracy, the kind of information we would need in order to begin our calculations, we need a starting point, and the starting point is when tourists arrive at the airport, or the railway station, or the ferry port, or perhaps through the Eurotunnel by road.

At this point, the tourists have only paid their fare to come here, and have not begun spending anything within the so-called United Kingdom, yet we are in vague territory already, 'scuse pun (territory).

Each and every tourist would need to be questioned, to establish how much they had paid to get here, and so whether they had used monies that were going to benefit the British economy financially rather than businesses in other countries.

It would be necessary to find out whether they were attracted to the country by the monarchy or not, would they have come anyway, or would they be in the 'middle space' where they would come to see Royal sites regardless of whether the Royal Family was actually in existence or not, whether the buildings, estates, lands, would have been of interest anyway, just by themselves, as that would not be able to be included.

The only ways to gather such data are to personally question every tourist, or to have them complete a very detailed and precise questionnaire, which would then require the necessary numbers of people and the processing systems to evaluate, and that would differ every year which would mean that a one-off calculation would not be permanent and so would be unsatisfactory anyway.

The alternative to those two options is to make assumptions, guesses, at applicable proportions of their spends, to estimate the results that might have been gathered, though the variables are already beginning to mount up and such assumptions are themselves, already, too inaccurate to be of any functional use.

Guesses with no precedent or data to guide us, and we are at the earliest and most straightforward step; assumptions this early on, mean that we are already acting without actual values and attracting inaccuracies from the very beginning.

We guess the total amounts of tourists using each travel method.

We guess the total amounts the tourists paid in fares.

We guess the proportions of the monies spent, on fares alone at this juncture, that ended up in the coffers of British companies.

We guess the percentages of tourists that would answer in each category as regards the specific reasons for coming to Britain.

Look how many guesses, and therefore inaccuracies, we are introducing, and none of the tourists have even started spending within the so-called United Kingdom yet.

Unless we do actually interview every tourist face to face, by their millions, which is obviously logistically not possible, and even if we did, we would still have to apportion assumptions to a number of the proportions of all the relevant measurements.

As they begin to spend, the next unworkable process would then have to be …………

We follow every single tourist for the duration of their holiday, logging exactly how much they spend on everything that they do, eat, drink, pay an entrance fee for, pay for accommodation, and at the end of the holiday we add it all up and get a full total of their spend.

Once again I am obviously referring to a method of gathering our data that is logistically impossible to carry out.

Or of course we could just guess all of those numbers as well, on top of all the variables that we have already been guessing.

That constitutes guesses on top of guesses, and our figures are going to be useless, so adversely approximated and compromised that there would be not a microbe of accuracy through any of it.

So, if we want the best possible approximation of accuracy, and there is no point in attempting this otherwise even though we would still have to involve much guesswork, we would have no alternative but to employ millions of staff to shadow every tourist for their entire visit - again logistically impossible, and nobody would seriously conceive that approach as viable, but I really do have to be careful about making anything complicated when so many lies are in play.

Not to mention, the financial cost of paying the people that are gathering that data, billions of pounds, is now a colossal new and additional financial outlay brought to bear on the calculations, compounding everything to a separate level, and it would then be a different calculation to that of prior years!

I hope the insane ludicrousness of the whole argument is now presenting itself.

If I am sounding at all sarcastic and silly, it is because the whole matter is silly.

If there wasn't a stupid, and deliberately misleading, narrative perpetuating an absolutely impossible assertion in the first place, on the basis of it being a fact when it isn't, nor is it possible to calculate or get anywhere close to being measurable, then I wouldn't be writing this section at all, or feeling that I need to.

People of course actually travel to Britain for a huge array of reasons.

They come to see ancient monuments such as Stonehenge, or to watch their German or Dutch football team play a match against a British team in a European tournament, or some to see Buckingham Palace or Balmoral and Windsor Castles without the slightest interest in the actual existence of the Royal Family whatsoever, because it is well within the realms of possibility to be interested purely in the architecture, plus it is not as if a tourist is ever able to get even a glimpse of a member of the illustrious family anyway.

Other tourists will come to visit the Lake District, or the Scottish Highlands, or the Hebrides, or Snowdonia, or the august magnificence of the colleges of the world-renowned universities of Oxford and Cambridge, or our many awe-inspiring cathedrals, churches and castles.

Or, simply, just to visit relatives or friends.

They themselves might, perhaps, be of the opinion that a monarchy is an obscene beacon of rampant and ruthless inequality; that 500 homeless people could in theory live in the vacant unused rooms of Buckingham Palace; or that a liquidation of the Royal Family's assets i.e. land, castles, investments, assets in secret bank accounts in, say, Switzerland, Jersey and the Cayman Islands, and every other sneaky tax haven where stashes are hidden by the wealthy, the big stolen diamonds and jewels, and any other possessions, all shared out, could pull every single British family and individual out of poverty, and so those particular tourists might feel that coming because of the monarchy is the very last possible motive for coming to this so-called United Kingdom.

The British people, one way or another over the years, bought everything anyway, didn't they?

Therefore all the required numbers are completely immeasurable, and so it is unknown, and it always will be, whether the monarchy pays for itself or not; I dared not miss out a step for obvious reasons…..phew.

So when anybody claims it to be true, it is a crass, absolute lie out of ignorance, and only said in order that people with no understanding of such an investigation will believe it, because it sounds like it could possibly be true and accurately correct to those of limited aptitude for logical perception.

As usual it is the lower intellectual strata that are being treated with utter contempt, and being expected to follow a pseudo-intellectual, royalist, crook, liar, with a believable, to the ignorant and gullible, voice, and posh name and/or title - though a title is by no means any guarantee of wisdom, intelligence, knowledge, honesty or integrity - to get behind this pathetic lie like so many blind sheep.

Anybody, from this day forward, that wishes to convince anybody of the veracity of the myth - try and PROVE IT - which can't be done - rather than insult everyone's intelligence, making a wishy-washy, unspecific, comment with no basis.

That is the end of explaining that, but regardless of all the arguments for and against the monarchy, it's important to be fair.

…….

Our Royal Family can't help being descendants of original Kings and Queens that became monarchs in the conventional fashion, namely killing more people than anyone else and then appointing themselves as monarchs.

We can't blame them for that, they were just born.

I feel some sympathy for some of them, particularly our newest golden, celebrity Royal couples, namely the Duke and Duchess of Cambridge and the Duke and Duchess of Sussex, with those sweet invented titles, whom I will be rigorously defending, you may be surprised to hear, in an upcoming passage.

For example, while it must be pleasant and comfortable to know that however many children one has, they will all grow up to be Princes and Princesses with automatic wealth and unearned privilege, to never need to want for anything material, due to bottomless finances paid for by all the subservient minions, there is the downside of living in what are effectively ornate prison cells.

Admittedly those prison cells are far more opulent and ornamental than those inhabited by actual lawbreakers, but a similarly imprisoned and heavily restricted life nonetheless.

Being able to wander anonymously around Harrods, Marks & Spencer, Asda or Poundland, without being mobbed by the peasant population, or relentless crowds of photographers, is, I guess, underrated when thought about in that context.

Also Prince Andrew, the Duke of York, with his 10,000 men marching up and down the hill behind him, is unfairly treated with the use of the cruel nickname 'Air Miles Andy' due to his keenness to travel by expensive-yet-free helicopters.

Why unfairly, you ask?

Is it just unjust in theory, you ask?

Nay, I have irrefutable, first-hand, cast-iron proof.

It is just unjust in practice as well as in theory.

Pray tell, my liege.

Indeed I shall.

He is currently the Chancellor of the University of Huddersfield.

I attended the graduation ceremony of a friend, who was expecting to receive a handshake from him, but in fact the Grand Old Duke of York was not even in attendance.

And that is in spite of the fact that the helicopter ride from London is only an hour or so in duration.

This proves, beyond all doubt, that he does not necessarily use expensive-yet-free helicopters, at every opportunity and excuse, at all.

My friend was met, instead, with the announcement that "the Duke of York congratulates the graduates", and the bizarre ritual of a shiny sceptre being laid on a table at the front of the hall for the entirety of the ceremony.

Fortunately, there were plenty of common, but authentic, academics and officials that were able to step in and shake the hands of the graduates, and so all was well.

Therefore It is important to be fair to the Royals, because they seem to go through a lot more heartache and trauma than it first appears.

......

One does hope that they do at least pay for themselves, while our country is so short of money, due to the absence of both 1) a Magic Money Tree and 2) a sensible and progressive economic strategy, which I will also scrutinise shortly.

It is a crying shame that the calculation cannot be done, but at least I hope that nobody now attempts to insult our collective intelligence and lie to us about it in future, it is very unscrupulous and deceitful to mislead people but it is no longer possible on this topic.

The Movers & Shakers
(the 'Oxford phenomenon')

Before addressing all the current matters and personnel that are relevant to present-day affairs, I feel it hugely relevant to point out some very interesting pieces of information about politicians of recent years, because the trends are glaring, yet not common knowledge. I first want to list certain persons along with the universities that they attended, along with the subjects they studied as undergraduates:

Theresa May - St. Hugh's College, Oxford - Geography.
David Cameron - Brasenose College, Oxford - 'PPE' (Philosophy, Politics and Economics).
Boris Johnson - Balliol College, Oxford - Classics.
Jacob Rees-Mogg - Trinity College, Oxford - History.
George Osborne - Magdalen College, Oxford - Modern History.
Tony Blair - St. John's College, Oxford - Jurisprudence (Law).
(+ best buddies Alastair Campbell - Gonville & Caius College, Cambridge - Modern Languages, and Peter Mandelson - St, Catherine's College, Oxford - PPE).
Michael Gove - Lady Margaret Hall, Oxford - English.

Others of note:
Gordon Brown - University of Edinburgh - History.
Margaret Thatcher (nee Roberts) - Somerville College, Oxford - Chemistry - though she was actually rejected and was only offered a place due to someone else's withdrawal.

However, one must remember, critically, that she will have been competing against the brains of other science students rather than the brains of linguists and historians. Draw whatever conclusion you wish from that, but my implication is obvious enough. It was my subject after all. I am (half) joking there.

Nigel Farage did not attend any university, as you would almost certainly have assumed. I am not aware of any degree courses in Pompous Shouting And Insulting Cleverer People.

As you can see with very little perceptive ability, with the exception of Mrs. Thatcher who barely achieved a place, two things. One, almost everyone attended the University of Oxford, only Alastair Campbell and Gordon Brown are exceptions. Two, there are no scientists or mathematicians whatsoever other than Margaret Thatcher. There is history, geography, law, and that curious animal 'PPE'. The undergraduates and alumni of Oxford know well what esteem the course of philosophy, politics & economics is held in. A certain very famous mouse, by the name of Mickey, studied the subject back in the 1940s, and due to his celebrity his name stuck with it and became synonymous with it. I'm making that up, obviously, he is a cartoon and two-dimensional (flat). I'm being mischievous. I will just safely and diplomatically say that among the students, it is not considered one of the courses that any of the cleverest echelons of people study. Although, no doubt, there will be content that has relevance to those that wish to become career politicians, that most elevated of human aspirations. Though ironically, much as I think like a scientist, these passages do contain fragments of philosophy, and politics, and economics.

I have insinuated, without much subtlety, that advanced logical capability is not part of the skill set of politicians usually, and so that is why logical thoughts and insights see things that politicians don't.

I must also, again, level the observation that television/radio/newspaper interviews do not uncover or come from angles that they sometimes should, and that is either a limitation of interviewers or the agreement that particular questions are not to be asked, or possibly both. Such deals about the content of interviews are, I am reliably told, commonplace. What else would we expect from politicians if we are being honest?

To be somewhat more specific, it seems that whenever I see or hear the words of politicians, journalists or commentators, or the parts of their discourse which editors allow through, they are absolutely riddled with hypocrisy, inconsistencies and contradictions. The logical progression of further questioning is almost always absent.

I have never once in my entire life encountered a mathematician or a scientist that had the tiniest, remotest aspiration to become a politician. I can't claim they don't exist but I've never met one. If you are a mathematician or a scientist yourself reading this, you will not be needing an explanation of why that is the case. Mostly, what are affectionately known as the 'aristocrat spawn' at Oxford harbour such ambitions, and they invariably study history, or classics, or the infamous, good old PPE. Occasionally English. The word 'aristocrat' has a number of definitions, but that is not important because it is just a collective term of endearment and so no further specifics are necessary. Anyway, they are big fans of networking - it's who you know as people say - but ironically, one can be sure that the ultra-exclusive Bullingdon Club would have any invitation, that members would proudly, and self-gratifyingly, and with a gleeful air of old money entitlement, never issue to anyone from a state school, robustly torn up and pissed on if they tried it. That's guesswork on my part, since of course I haven't ever seen someone from a state school invited to the said club. It might perhaps be a surprise to 'them' to find out that 'common' people, too, also have not the slightest interest in spending time with 'their kind', though the approximately 100,000 reasons why would clearly take far too long to list. Certainly spending time with the likes of David Cameron, George Osborne and Boris Johnson creates a picture akin to the concept of purgatory. Stewart Lee's routine about his Oxford undergraduate friendship with David Cameron is a highly interesting and hilarious angle on the subject. And it makes those 100,000 reasons ever so easy to work out. So they have their class snobbery while the common people have their intellectual snobbery, which one could easily argue is a far more powerful and meaningful form of snobbery. The shallow and pompous caricatures of elitism, who seem to strut around in apparent blissful ignorance of the fact they come across in that way, both as students as well as later in life, have a big, fat zero in common with those capable of studying subjects that demand higher - no, let's be generous and diplomatic and just say different - cerebral aptitudes.

74

In a similar vein, I did not hesitate to refuse two approaches during my professional career to join different lodges of Freemasons. It seemed that in a similar way I was supposed to feel flattered and privileged, but I didn't. The reasons that people involve themselves with such organisations, can be, just as equally, reasons not to. I didn't have any spare time anyway, I always worked long hours and also had a family as it was, but I doubt that it would have made any difference to my responses. I felt no longing for acceptance, which seemed to be the key reason for association with them. And there were no women, how boring.

....

It should, then, come as no surprise that we in the so-called United Kingdom find ourselves having to deal with a self-serving Establishment, that contains individuals with zero accountability, with zero relevant experience and qualifications despite being employed to do crucial work, due to being appointed for all the wrong reasons.

One of the many forms of the abuse of power, therefore. In stark contrast to pragmatic, objective thinkers, like one would be far more likely to encounter within the private sector, where the primary motivator is the delivery of results, would appoint the right woman, or man, for the role in question by means of their attributes to carry out the work. The right qualifications, experience, and evidence of previous relevant success, rather than a university drinking and vomiting buddy that has none of those things in their arsenal - in a 'jobs for the boys' arrangement.

75

We end up with the Far Left, the Far Right and the Far Wrong, within a hierarchy devoid of sagacity, wisdom, common sense, balance, logic and integrity.

Not to mention the bad decisions, and the inappropriate policies, that inevitably result from such a deeply flawed system with its irrational and dishonest functionality.

It is often said that politicians become politicians because they can't do anything else, which I do not actually agree with. I think that there are, indeed, undoubtedly many that can't do anything else, but there are also those who can't even 'do' politics as well as not being able to do anything else. There are lots of them in Parliament right now who display complete incompetence, and talk nothing but absolute drivel, and stating their names is not necessary since we all know exactly who they are.

To close, a practical observation to summarise this passage.

Politicians that are not accountable for the delivery of actual results, are usually the most avid of analysts, and the loudest critics, of those that are.

That is precisely why the great majority of them do not belong in the private sector. Big on words and loving the sound of their own voices, but no need to do anything that requires an advanced and appropriate set of skills and experience. They do not possess the qualities for it, and so would not perform well enough to survive.

The NHS (Pt. 1)
Compulsions v. Consequences

We make choices at almost
every moment of our lives.

Nobody compels us to smoke a cigarette,
except perhaps the peer pressure from our 'friends'
to try the first one.
I say that for the benefit of those with
poor mental powers
to make sensible decisions,
like saying "no" or "fuck off".
Every cigarette is a choice, a decision.
Every single one.
A choice to either smoke it, or not to,
unless it is smoked passively,
in the case of a baby or a child, perhaps.
This can be ably illustrated
by the story of my early childhood,
when both of my parents
smoked heavily in our home,
treating my sisters and I to
copious quantities of free nicotine.

At that time though,
the full dangers were much less known.
You would think that if I survived all of that
concentrated passive smoking,
my sisters and I would have an automatic habit,
yet miraculously I grew up
with a hatred of the nicotine, and the tar,
and the smell of the smoke
and also even of unlit tobacco itself.
My sisters are non-smokers too.

The downside being it did also cause me to
push away my parents
when they tried to give me hugs.
Which is saddening.

The magnetism of addiction in my case
worked in opposite,
fortunately, yet even as a toddler,
my rejection was based just as much on the logic
of not developing a stupid, pathetic dependency
on a stupid plant
that costs a rather silly amount of money, and which
would make my breath, clothes and house smell
worse than a heap of pig shit,
and also, more trivially, as a bonus,
might well end my life.

I only had to make the one good decision
instead of 20 bad ones per day.

----.

Nobody forces us to drink a pint of beer.
Nobody forces us to drink a double shot of vodka.
Nobody forces us to get so drunk
that we can't speak properly,
or walk properly,
or see properly, yet
we might make the sufficient number of
bad decisions in an evening to
achieve all of the above.
Subsequent to that extremely idiotic achievement,
nobody forces us to start a fight that puts us
in an ambulance and an Accident & Emergency
department, or worse.

Just lifestyle choices, that's all.
Maybe in that self-inflicted, dysfunctional state
we make a catastrophically bad decision,
and drive a car straight into somebody
that has made no relevant decisions at all -
which causes them to arrive
in an A & E department by ambulance,
because a drunk driver has ploughed into them.

The wrong place at the wrong time for them,
no lifestyle choice for them to cause their injuries
and, often, subsequent death.
The driver's decisions did the job, very well, instead.
Maybe the piss-head driver hit another car,
from being so incapacitated
that he, or she, was turning a blind corner
on the wrong side of the road.
Maybe there were four people in that other car,
and maybe none of them survived it.
Perhaps the car ploughed into a tree, or a wall.
I had my unmanned car murdered in cold blood,
written off by a drunk woman,
while parked right outside my front door.
She was unable to speak or walk when she tried to.

Those are all just
hypothetical,
imaginary
situations of course.
Fictional. Made up.
Like God, money, or ownership of land.

Fortunately, hospitals are places where science is
obeyed and not religion,
so that more people get better, faster.

79

Anyway, as illustrated, the wrong
choices can give rise to
cataclysmic outcomes.
Perhaps, instead, just 10 inebriated morons,
in a brawl, with a few broken glasses in hand,
and any number of the possible bad happenings
occur.
Any number ending up in the ambulance
and then the A & E department,
where the medical professionals
try to salvage the lives that they can manage to,
while they all lose substantial quantities of blood.

…….

Nobody physically compels us to eat,
our bodies tell us when to eat, don't they?
Do they?

Let's examine the lifestyle choices involved in this.

Who forces us to walk through the door of
a fast food restaurant?
Each time, every time? With our children?
Who forces us to eat a bar of chocolate,
or perhaps two bars? Three? Four?
Who forces us to buy tubs of ice cream
at the supermarket?
Who orders us to buy cheese,
or pizzas covered in cheese?
Conscious decisions, day, after day, after day.

Ice cream, cheese, and chocolate contain, of course,
a high concentration of saturated fats.
The building blocks of furred arteries and
heart disease.

Anyone that knows no such nutritional information
can look in the mirror once in a while,
where there are big, fat, non-cryptic clues.
Who is it that forces us to eat as much food again
as the amount we had eaten when we felt full up?
Who stopped us from stopping?
Why did we do no exercise to burn excess calories?
Every single mouthful is a decision.

A decision not to go to the gym, or run up the road,
is as much a decision as one to go to the gym or run
up the road.

―.―

The more bad decisions we make,
and tho more frequently we make them,
over time,
constitute a lifestyle.
Yet at any moment, of any hour, of any day,
we can make different - better - decisions.
If we make enough of those
better decisions, we have a different
lifestyle, with different outcomes.

It's all optional, it's all voluntary.

Every decision, every choice.

…….

If I switch from elementary logic to an opinion,
wrapped up in a question…….

Why should people
that have made enough stupid decisions,
over a significant enough period
that they are on the brink of death,

81

or seriously ill for a significant period of time
and so are using large quantities of NHS resources,
<u>not</u> be told,
"we're very sorry, but your condition was
a consequence of your lifestyle choices.
Choices that you, at any time, could have stopped
or done something about,
and so - unfortunately -
you must either be denied treatment altogether,
or be treated <u>after</u> all the patients
that did not cause or contribute to
their reasons for needing help.

If you're still 'with us' at that point!"

Is there any valid, counter-argument whatsoever?
"Smokers pay tax on their cigarettes"
is much more an endorsement of their stupidity
than a valid reply to the question.

If a government refuses to fully fund healthcare
because there is no Magic Money Tree
(at least for such trivial priorities,
since there needs to be a pot for
essential vote-purchasing bribes,
and the latest state-of-the-art
extra-lethal nuclear warheads),
then such vital matters, that take precedent
over human suffering,
that make waiting lists a fact of life,
surely dictate that
the waiting lists be appropriately ordered?

With self-inflicted irresponsibility at the bottom?

I hear many cerebrally impaired people,
either through their own lack of ability to think,
or in believing racist poison
which has permeated our society so much
that it could have been accessed anywhere,
that try to perpetuate
the entirely false narrative;

"Immigration places too much pressure on the NHS".

I've just carefully explained why the NHS is really
under pressure.

They say one-third of ex-pats
are planning to return to live in the
so-called United Kingdom.
They can't, can they, surely?
An ex-pat must use at least as many resources
as an immigrant (a refugee in fact)?
Many of them are quite elderly,
they'd use more.
But no, there's no issue with that scenario,
my logic is fundamentally flawed.
I had forgotten to factor in skin colour.
…...

The sad thing is,
people such as those racist specimens,
such venomous, uninformed, misinformed pigs,
could read what I have written
a million times,
and not only would they not be able to
compute and understand the contents,
but they wouldn't want to.
It would erase their scapegoats and their bigotry.

Then they would no doubt have a smoke,
and a few drinks,
and turn their conversations to
the unwelcome foreigners, that are also to blame for
everything else that's wrong with the
so-called United Kingdom,
then quickly onto the subject of football, or big ends.
Strangely, I was in no doubt at all that the racists
without brain cells, or GCSEs
were the actual disease of our society,
given a helping hand by the other scourge,
the readily available and affordable,
rampant, unchecked
Propaganda.

And so, hospitals are full of people
that have literally chosen to be there.
And since the NHS is both
underfunded and understaffed,
while being both
overcrowded and overstretched,
it is impossible to conclude any piece on this subject
without a small mention for the
Right Honourable Jeremy Hunt.

I find I have to concentrate to use the
correct spelling of his surname
instead of the more appropriate one.
Punt.

He's the man who decided to mitigate the
scandalous cuts to budgets
by forcing staff, that were already working at levels
that unnecessary deaths had occurred,
to work under a contract

that made them agree to work for longer.
He held the trump card, because of course
people who devote their own lives
to saving the lives of other people,
would not strike and endanger their patients
whilst he, conversely,
appeared not to give a sparrow's shit
about the patients
or the professionals.
A manager, whose management style
consists of blaming anyone but himself for
everything.
Which, of course, is not a management style,
or management at all
let alone anything approaching leadership.
It is the opposite of good management, because
management is about ownership of,
and responsibility for,
everything that goes on within one's
designated area.
Now can you see how a politician
would be unable to do it?
A perfect example of what I said
such a short while ago.

He tried to defend the out-of-date
hardware and software
that hospital administration and databases rely on,
when the entire system was
compromised and crashed.

I just feel that sometimes,
things in general aren't thought through.
I realise some people aren't able to think things
through.

85

Jeremy Hunt attended Magdalen College, Oxford – PPE.

No, I wasn't surprised either.

It makes one wonder, how many better candidates,
with more appropriate experience and capabilities,
might a real recruitment process have found?

As with all the other named Oxford Alumni,
except myself obviously,
he will, in due course,
regardless of ability or achievement,
follow his time as a Cabinet minister
with a knighthood,
and spend the rest of his life
as a member of the House Of Lords.

Let us hope that he has a long, healthy life
and not need to have
too much medical treatment along the way.

I'm joking.

He'll have private medical insurance.

If I appear to have too much bitterness on show,
it is, I expect, just me needing psychiatric help,
due to my lifestyle choice of
excessive critical thinking.

'This is based on true events.'

Like many other people, for very powerful and justified personal reasons that I do not care to share, I am angry at the tobacco plant. But more than my hatred for the plant, since the plant is, after all, only a plant, without a brain, I despise to my very core the immoral (I was going to say 'maggots' but I suppose it's a bit rude) in tobacco companies that think that it's OK to still sell the stuff to people, and to recruit children worldwide into using their addictive substances. I also despise the (I was going to say 'cockroach' but I suppose it's a bit rude) politicians that do not have the balls to legislate to ban nicotine permanently from all our lives. They do not do that because it's a taxed product, and brings in cold, hard cash. Plus what is deceitfully and inaccurately termed 'lobbying'. I would also not be at all surprised if money changes hands in inappropriate ways. No different than buying votes which is, it seems, perfectly acceptable and legal behaviour. So long as it's British politicians doing it, otherwise it's criminal and makes big headlines within the machinery of Propaganda.

Is it pitiful or comical to see the little groups of people huddled outside workplaces, wrapped up against the freezing cold, to get a nicotine fix in the winter?

Personally I think it is both highly pitiful
and highly comical.

P.A.T.H.E.T.I.C.

Does it not occur to those drug addicts - for that is precisely what they are - that their bodies do not wake them up two or three times in the night, breaking their sleep, in order to gain fixes of nicotine? Their bodies

87

cope perfectly well with a night's sleep without topping up their poison levels. Defeating addictions might be aided by nicotine patches, gum or tablets, but in the final analysis, addictions are defeated by the mind. Willpower alone will easily achieve it if in correct focus, and without any willpower no solution will work.

It is nothing more than whether a mind is strong or weak.

Drugs, also, I recall, are supposed to be illegal.

Respect and congratulations are due to the parents who help to, by example, educate their children to grow up as smokers, a.k.a. nicotine addicts, and/or set them on a path to obesity, diabetes and heart attacks. Regular visits to fast food outlets and shoving something under their kids' noses some 30 seconds or so later, do save the effort of cooking meals though.

There are 'vaping' shops everywhere nowadays.

Why is it not a surprise to see smokers make a decision to substitute a known killer substance, plus all the additives, for something with absolutely no long term test results available to find out whether it will also threaten their lives? That is simply a case of replacing one ignorant practice with a different one.

"But I need to do something with my hands".

Then learn to knit or play the oboe.

The NHS (Pt. 2)
Tobacco Road

I was happy with the few anti-tobacco comments I had made in Part 1, which I had regarded as the end of my NHS passage, until perchance I stumbled across something that stunned me and amused me greatly, and it gave birth to Part 2.

Reference: The Independent, Friday 10 August 2018.

Andy Martin meets Peter Nixon (Managing Director, Philip Morris).

Philip Morris International, one of the largest tobacco companies in the world, is running a campaign entitled 'Hold My Light', the purpose of which is to encourage smokers worldwide to stop smoking. But before one gets too carried away, there is much to examine. However, it is clearly a headline-grabbing piece of marketing, even without advertisements on the front pages of newspapers, which also occurs. Read on.

Although the article reads, I think, like a piece of fawning teenage fan-mail, which if you have read it will not have escaped your notice, it is an interesting exercise to go through it objectively and analyse it.

First though, tobacco companies can hardly be called bastions of morality. Nowadays it is well-known, backed up by millions upon millions of medical cases and data, that smoking tobacco causes cancers, heart disease, strokes, lung diseases, diabetes, chronic obstructive pulmonary disease and others, in fact it harms nearly every organ of the body. And in the so-called United Kingdom in 2015, tobacco smoking caused an estimated 115,000 deaths. That was 19% of all deaths. In the USA, it causes more than 480,000 deaths annually. Worldwide, the figure is almost 6 million per year, and the estimate is that it will be 8 million by 2030.

From the CDC (Centers for Disease Control and Prevention) Fact Sheet for 2018, more than 16 million Americans are living with a disease caused by smoking. For every person who dies because of smoking, at least 30 others live with a serious smoking-related illness. It causes tuberculosis, some eye diseases, immune system problems and rheumatoid arthritis, and erectile dysfunction in males. Luckily not in females though. It is the primary cause of preventable deaths. Smokers die on average 10 years younger than non-smokers. I could go on, and on, and on, but Google and Bing are there should anyone want the full picture.

In any case, Philip Morris International was founded in the year 1900, but it was not until 1999 that it was prepared to openly state that there was a link between cigarette smoking and all of the horrible medical conditions that it is a cause of. Even then, they and all of the other major tobacco companies were extremely careful not to be too specific about any link between their company's products specifically to the risks and dangers. And that is because, the great many attempted lawsuits against tobacco companies in the past were defended, invariably successfully, by making sure that exceptions and loopholes were still there to be exploited to avoid being held accountable for all of the deaths and illnesses that they might be, and/or have been, sued for.

Lines of defence that have been used successfully to prevent large compensation payments to people with severe and often terminal medical conditions include:

1) There being no scientific proof that cigarette smoking causes lung cancer (earlier cases). Not used in later cases once awareness of this issue increased.
2) The plaintiff not having lung cancer as claimed.
3) The plaintiff having a type of lung cancer not associated with cigarette smoking.
4) The plaintiff having cancer that may have been associated with cigarette smoking or smokeless tobacco use, but tobacco products were not to blame in this specific case.
5) The plaintiff having cancer that may have been associated with cigarette smoking, but the defendant's cigarette brands were not to blame.
6) The defendant's cigarettes, or smokeless tobacco, may have played a role in the plaintiff's illness or death, but other risk factors were present that negated or mitigated the defendant's responsibility.
7) The defendant's cigarettes may have been a factor in the plaintiff's illness or death, but the plaintiff knew
8) of the health risks and exercised free will in choosing to smoke and declining to quit.

Much as I am highly cynical of tobacco companies in all manner of ways, I also completely sympathise with the 'free will' argument of defence now that we are in an age where the negative effects of smoking are common knowledge. Just because a substance is addictive is not any excuse, in my opinion, for starting or continuing to use it. It can hardly be the fault of a tobacco company if someone has low, or no, willpower.

So it was 99 years of trading that Philip Morris managed to get under their belt before having to openly acknowledge the dangerous effects of their products. Other tobacco companies were similarly aligned. You couldn't say they have a history of pursuing health-promoting initiatives, or that they are counted among the ethical and honourable businesses of the world.

In fact tobacco was promoted for many years as being fashionable and 'cool' and even having health benefits - memorable examples being the "More Doctors Smoke Camels Than Any Other Cigarette" advertising campaign, containing the question "What Cigarette Do You Smoke, Doctor?" and describing the reason for their choice being the "mild, good tasting cigarette" that is a Camel. There was the "Little Katie Chewing Tobacco" advert from the late 19th Century which had a picture of a little girl on it. "Cigares De Joy Give Immediate Relief In Cases Of Asthma, Cough, Bronchitis, Hay-Fever, Influenza and Shortness of Breath". (Such a wonderful wording looked at it from our modern perspective and understanding!) Lucky Strike went with the Camels angle, with "20,679 Physicians saying Luckies are less irritating. It's toasted. Your throat protection against irritation". "St. Dunstan's Virginia" showed a child smoking, accompanied by "Don't Be Angry Daddy, it's for St. Dunstan's".

Granger's Pipe Tobacco proudly declared that "The Only Pipe Smoker Who Does Not Like It…..Is The One Who Never Tried It."

Philip Morris & Co in 1936 stated, literally, in its ad with a beaming red-jacketed boy holding a packet of cigarettes the size of his chest using both hands:

"Scientific Research Has, At Last, Enabled Philip Morris To Replace Personal Opinion With Scientific Fact: Philip Morris Cigarettes Have Been PROVED By Actual Tests On The Human Throat Measurably And Definitely Milder Than Ordinary Cigarettes. A Fact Ethically Presented To And Accepted By The Medical Profession. NO OTHER CIGARETTE CAN MAKE THIS STATEMENT!" America's Finest Cigarettes, 15c.

I'll stop with that, as we have a claim of scientifically proven health advantage within the newspaper article I spoke of before, by a representative of the same tobacco company, so we have come full circle.

…..…

I will therefore now return to the amusing content of Andy Martin's incredibly sycophantic piece of journalism.

He gives us some information about Mr. Nixon's appearance, he is apparently "young, fit and tanned", has white teeth rather than brown, and looks more like he runs a sports company than a tobacco company. Then a potted history, his parents were a policeman and a nurse, mentioned presumably to frame him as inherently respectable, he studied Japanese at Cardiff University and worked for Price Waterhouse in Japan. Mr. Martin makes no attempt to mask how impressed he is.

The article, remember, is about Philip Morris' campaign to get its customers to stop smoking, though without the slightest hint of subtlety, the narrative dovetails perfectly with promotion of Philip Morris' range of electronic cigarettes, branded IQOS. This activity is colloquially referred to as "vaping". And here comes the claim about the IQOS products; Mr. Nixon makes the claim that these products give a "90-95% risk reduction" when compared to tobacco products. Seamlessly we go from the impression of helping people, to the promotion of alternative products.

You would expect a journalist to immediately probe and quiz this claim for rigorous evidence and long-term scientific studies to compare like-for-like with cigarette tests, in order to claim such a huge advantage to switching. No such questions are asked and so no further information comes. It is stated as if it is fact, and poor Mr. Martin is too overawed and blown away that he leaves it for the reader to assume it is a fact.

This is the exact dynamic which demanded that I write this whole section.

Not even the young girl in the vaping shop closest to my home fell for my test, when I went in to discuss the pastime and got around to asking the questions about safety and health. I expected her to have been instructed to make unrealistic claims, but she was honest and spoke of the products being too recently developed to have had real, rigorous studies done and meaningful data gathered. David Nixon doesn't initially come across as being as transparent as Kirsty. He also comes from tobacco culture, so I am at least doubly suspicious.

If somebody wants to float the claim that something gives a 90-95% risk reduction, it jolly well needs some serious long-term evidence and data to back it up, and it is the job of a journalist, if they want to write objectively about such a bold assertion, to insist it is available, at least that is what I believe is required with a stated claim such as this one. But there is absolutely nothing of the sort in this piece. Taken at face value, and clearly intended to be accepted at face value by the reader. Mr. Nixon must have been overjoyed at such an easy ride, or was that again all agreed beforehand? Forgive my cynicism, but that certainly appears to be the case. I suppose I should seek out more familiarity with Mr. Martin's work and see what I find.

So, no evidence, no figures, no studies, no proof, but 90-95% risk reduction we are told. It must be true. Back to Mr. Martin and Mr. Nixon.

In Japanese, apparently, "the customer gets the highest level of respect", and Mr. Martin said he was of the view that "it felt like that in the IQOS store", which of course is the Philip Morris vaping shop, in case we forget. It is, according to Mr. Martin,"like an Apple shop". I assume he is referring to the computer manufacturer and not the fruit.

It is confusing me, is this an article or an advertisement? Actually it is not confusing at all, I know exactly how it is coming across.

How, as smokers, can we resist hot-footing it down to the IQOS outlet immediately to spend lots of money on these miraculous 90-95% safer nicotine products? In fact, as a non-smoker myself, it is very difficult to resist starting to vape with almost totally risk-free nicotine, I mean, 90-95% allegedly, what's the problem? I should indulge in the ultra-glamorous pastime without delay. Unless I first explore this a little bit more……
Mr. Martin and Mr. Nixon are bonding so well that I cannot hold back my inquisitive nature. And it seems just as well that I can't.

Is Mr. Nixon a pure altruist, trying to convert smokers to products which are, if we require no serious scientific involvement, 90-95% less risky because he says so? It soon becomes clear who we are dealing with.

"I want the 40-a-day Marlboro guy to walk in here." I bet you do.

Mr. Martin to the rescue; "he is genuinely concerned about existing smokers". I don't doubt Mr. Nixon has a silver tongue, but Mr. Martin is seemingly a salesman's dream. He continues; "his goal is to get millions of smokers to stop. I believe him." Just imagine sitting in Mr. Martin's front room on a wet Tuesday, discussing double glazing or a new driveway, what a perfect and profitable evening.

It's not over yet by a long chalk.

"Mr. Nixon is almost evangelical in his conviction."
"It's like going gluten-free."
"It's like driving an electric car with zero pollution."

Scrap the notion of asking for ridiculous health claims to be proven, we are into the realm of eco-metaphors now.

The Independent has been comfortable to associate its name and reputation with this piece of journalism. It is worth remembering that 'independent' and 'impartial' are entirely different words which have entirely different meanings.

And as if to add insult to injury to that very statement, it is hard not to collapse with uncontrollable giggles reading the final words that I will select from Mr. Martin's eulogy. He said "I'm not making a final judgement on the above" (and that is very wise, I suggest that is best left to independent scientists - and by that I do not mean employed by The Independent newspaper or by Philip Morris International - and factual data, over like-for-like periods of time to tobacco_products). And also because this piece is in fact crammed like sardines with Mr. Martin's eloquently expressed but biased opinions, rather than scientific scrutiny, as well as that good old unchallenged 90-95% declaration. He then states "and I remain strictly objective and detached", which is perhaps the most overtly ironic and humorous phrase of the entire story.

Move over all you millionaire stand-up comedians, the new King of Mirth has seemingly arrived.

Mr. Martin says, by way of conclusion to his precise, objective, high-level scientific analysis, that we have his permission to be "as skeptical as we like". Thanks for that, I have been, and I will.

———

But let's ignore the boyish enthusiasm, stop getting too bogged down with wild humanitarian rhetoric, and redress the balance with some real, actual facts.

Philip Morris International makes Marlboro cigarettes, and Marlboro cigarettes are the biggest selling brand in the world. Whether that is an example of sheer hypocrisy is a tough call, that I will treat with twig-spine cowardice and not try.

"You decide", as the Big Brother voice-over man would put it.

Even with the massive reductions in tobacco revenues worldwide, partly because of the fact that the product actually kills the customers, and also because everybody knows that and so either do not start to smoke in the first place or quit if they have started, Philip Morris was still ranked at number 108 in the Fortune 500 list of American corporations for 2018.

1) In 2017, Philip Morris International was named as Number 2 in the published Top 10 FMCG

(Fast Moving Consumer Goods, how apt) companies.

2) Their products are sold in over 200 countries.

3) In 2017, Philip Morris sold 234.25 billion cigarettes in Asia, and 84.22 billion cigarettes in Canada and Latin America.

4) The 2017 revenue of the company was $78.098 billion.

5) The company has assets of $38.6 billion, achieved from the sale of its largely dangerous product range.

6) 87% of the company's sales are from cigarettes.

7) Philip Morris still advertises and markets its lethal products in every country where it legally can.

8) Cigarettes are still highly addictive, and still cause terminal illnesses.

9) There are approximately 7,000 chemicals in tobacco smoke.

10) Of those, 250 are known to be harmful. They include hydrogen cyanide, carbon monoxide and ammonia.

11) 69 of the 250 can cause cancer.

12) In the so-called United Kingdom in 2015/2016, there were 474,000 admissions to hospitals with smoking-related conditions.

13) In 2015, 16% of all deaths in the so-called United Kingdom, amounting to 79,000 people, were from smoking-related conditions. In 2016/2017, 11% of mothers were recorded as smokers.

14) It has been almost 20 years since that admission by Philip Morris that smoking causes cancer. They are still, in 2019, marketing worldwide and selling billions upon billions of cigarettes every year. I think we can be forgiven for being highly cynical of campaigns by such a company when they state an aim to stop people smoking with a context of benevolence and saintly righteousness.

15) (Because the statistical evidence of the worldwide marketing of deadly substances hugely outweighs such altruistic claims).

16) Philip Morris could choose to stop marketing cigarettes completely and immediately, and they clearly are not taking that course of action.

17) On the Jeremy Vine show, on Radio 2 on the 2nd January 2019, the Philip Morris 'Hold My Light' campaign was featured. The representative that took part stated, a number of times, that vaping products were a lot safer than tobacco products. On this occasion there was no mention of the

infamous 90-95% risk reduction, and those are sufficiently impressive numbers that I expected them to be mentioned. One could perhaps deduce that the lack of reference to those figures, reflected a realisation that it is easy to challenge stated claims like that without rigorous studies and evidence. But, although Jeremy Vine did challenge his guest over the apparent hypocrisy of selling cigarettes worldwide while claiming to be trying to stop people smoking, and also the apparent cynicism of simply really aiming to get people to switch to other Philip Morris products instead, under the dubious claim of scientifically proven healthier alternatives, he did not once challenge that claim of vaping being healthier than cigarette smoking even without the 90-95% claim. Jeremy Vine does not usually miss something so glaringly obvious, which begs the question "Why?". The production team would be the best people to ask I would have thought. So Mr. Martin didn't challenge it, and Mr. Vine didn't challenge it. All the while, vaping is becoming more and more popular. I do not see the media showing much interest at all. I smell a very stinky rat.

Philip Morris is a tobacco company, and there are lots of other tobacco companies that behave similarly, so I have zero personal respect for all tobacco companies on principle. However I have specific things to say about this particular situation and its coverage in the written article and its level of bias.

All sorts of institutions are paying lip service to taking positions against smoking, and claiming to be doing things to reduce the number of people who indulge in the habit.

A) The Government of the so-called United Kingdom, some years ago now, banned smoking indoors at commercial premises. So smokers step outside and smoke there instead. The interiors of the premises are more pleasant, but I would assert that it has had a negligible effect on smoking statistics - but I have no scientific study or figures on the matter, and so I have no proof. That's an example of how I think it is best to state a view as a view, rather than create the illusion of a fact without evidence. As within the earlier part of this section and 'The Great British Fallacy', where examples of blatant misinformation are addressed. No lies from me.

If Mr. Nixon and Philip Morris International are able to produce irrefutable and rigorous independent scientific evidence to support their claims, I will be happy to apologise for saying that. I am confident that I need make no such statement about the subject matter of the 'Fallacy' section.

B) Taxes are added to the price of tobacco products more or less every year, and that has been the case for many years. These increments are very small and very gradual, and again they seem to only serve to bring in steadily increasing revenue to the Treasury and have no effect on smoker numbers, and that is corroborated by the fact that it is never even referred to as an anti-smoking measure.

C) The Daily Mirror, the only tabloid that I ever have any time for, since it is the only one which takes a socialist standpoint on major issues, the others being proudly Right-Wing and therefore giving the British Press a massive lean towards the Right in Propaganda content, has chosen to tie its colours to the Philip Morris campaign. I doubt it's an accident that the front page - discounted, probably, but still very lucrative for the publication - has been adorned with Philip Morris advertising content, but some editorial sycophancy has also been printed. Of course, there has been nothing to challenge the lack of meaningful information about vaping anywhere in sight there either.

D) There is such a thing as the Tobacco Control Plan, which the so-called United Kingdom's Government is implementing in order to make the country "smoke-free in the next few decades", which is as vague and woolly as anything referred to in any part of the passages I've written. However some specifics have been quoted; the aim is apparently to reduce the smoking population from 15.5% to 12% by 2022. I'm trying not to laugh at how silly and unambitious that appears.

E) I'll have a punt at advising the people involved in that project how to smash the target to smithereens, knowing without a shadow of a doubt that my advice will not be followed, and I'll have a second punt at suggesting why it won't.

Governments worldwide could ban cigarettes completely and totally. Single nations could apply it unilaterally but it would not work, multilaterally it would work quite well, and that even if e-cigarettes were not touched by the ban.

Ever so simple but also a 0% probability of happening. The sheer volume of business, and therefore money, that the tobacco industry generates means that it holds significant influence at the highest levels. My suggestion is therefore not a serious one, I am an idealist to a point, but I'm enough of a pragmatist not to expect anything so ridiculous to be entertained at all.

Tobacco plantations provide a great many jobs in poorer countries, which also would cause havoc in the communities involved if they were to disappear, and so they won't be touched.

Corporate offices of tobacco companies, workers in the factories where cigarettes are manufactured and packaged, are all staffed with large numbers of employees that are also ring-fenced against any suggestion so radical.

The huge amounts of income and corporation tax payable by these industrial giants, in addition to the huge taxation revenues from cigarette sales, are also not going to be touched by governments for obvious reasons.

The 'black markets' would certainly be offered up by politicians as a reason - an excuse - for the unfeasibility of such an idea. Unilateral implementation of any bans would immediately create black markets from other countries, that is obvious. So multilateral implementation is the only way to eliminate the entire product. Also, black markets exist already, so the element of their effect has nothing to do with any ban whether it were unilateral or multilateral. The reason that black markets are a problem has nothing to do with consumers, consumers get their tobacco cheaper through black markets - but black markets bypass taxation, and so the Treasury departments suffer the reduction in revenue. And so governments are the ones who do not want black markets to operate.

'Big Tobacco', big business, big influence, big money.

The Michael Mann film 'The Insider' (1999) starring Russell Crowe, Al Pacino and Christopher Plummer, is the fictionalisation of a true story, and is about a tobacco company whistleblower (Crowe) that tries to get his story out into the public domain through a 60 Minutes reporter (Pacino). The way that the corporate machinations operate, along with the intense pressure that is placed on Crowe and his family, make for a gripping thriller which received 7 Academy Award nominations. It gives some insight into the ruthlessness of the industry.

It is, also, always worth remembering that Philip Morris advertisement from 1936 claiming scientific proof of the superiority of their products over others.

The absolute bottom line is this.

Morality, and the health and welfare of human beings, are no match for the sheer power of money, and that is a universal truth of capitalism. And whilst the tobacco industry is certainly a very accurate reflection of that statement, a great many industries and companies are equally shameful examples of the same principle.

Yet I honestly believe the last line of the next of these passages.

Pandora's Box

The Greek myth of Pandora's Box reads, simplistically, thus:

The titan Prometheus stole fire from Zeus, and gave it to mankind to help it to become civilised and to enable it to progress. By way of punishment, Prometheus was bound to a rock, and an eagle would feast on his liver each day. Overnight it would grow back, the punishment therefore to be repeated for eternity. This is similar to the punishment given to the King Sisyphus, whose fate was to push a huge boulder to the top of a hill. Shortly before reaching the summit, the boulder would roll back to the bottom. Therefore Sisyphus' ordeal also would repeat without end.

Pandora, a charming but deceitful woman, was given as a gift from Zeus to Prometheus' brother Epimetheus. She was made by the gods Athena and Hephaestus and was the first human woman, breathed into life by the four winds on Zeus' instructions, and would marry Epimetheus. She was given possession of a box, (literal translation: jar) which contained all the evils of the world, as a wedding present. She was instructed never to open it, though Zeus knew full well she would not be able to follow that instruction because he also blessed - or cursed - her with curiosity.

Inevitably the curiosity overcame her and she opened the box, and all the evils of the world were released, and unleashed, upon mankind. Out they all flew: Hate - War - Deceit - Violence - Jealousy - Anger - Despair - Spite - Aggression - Malevolence - Cruelty.

107

She tried to close the box quickly but the damage was done, and irreversibly so. Once the contents of the box escaped, there was no way of returning them to captivity and the effects on mankind were then permanent. The only thing that remained within the box was Hope.

The legend is now used to describe any act that brings about negative consequences that are irreversible, which is why I wish to use it as an analogy for a specific phenomenon, though in my case it refers to an irreversible change which has also great positives as well as its great negatives.

The Pandora's Box I refer to,
is the cornucopia that we call the Internet.

---·

The Internet is so much a part of our lives,
that it is incredible to think that
it has really only been with us,
in mainstream use,
for less than 20 years or so.
Bill Gates, speaking of starting Microsoft
with Paul Allen,
reminisces that they had talked and dreamed of
"a computer in every home"
and, of course,
"all of them running Microsoft software".
The dream actually became a reality,
and Mr. Gates became a multi-billionaire -
though entrepreneurs beware.
Mr. Gates' dream was about the innovation
and not the resulting wealth.

He gives away fortune after fortune to
charitable causes.

Today, we have a world that has been
enhanced a million-fold
by this invention, this innovation, this development.
This jamboree.
This 'World Wide Web'.

Not only that, but our connections to this
revolutionary endowment
are invisible.
No need for cables, nor physical connections,
but all around us an ether of cyberspace,
everywhere.
Is it real, actual magic? Something so incredible?

This phenomenon gives us:
all the wisdom and information
of every library in every country of the world,
just mouse-clicks away.
Anything we might wish to find out about
is simply a question of typing a word or phrase
into a search bar, and pressing 'Enter'.

The subject of our curious investigation,
within a couple of seconds,
is revealed.
A revolution in access to information.

A worldwide retail marketplace
is now at our fingertips,
we do not need to move from our armchairs
to purchase virtually anything we wish.
Billions of pounds changing hands every day.

109

Only needing to walk into an actual building
if we want to smell the scents of fragrances perhaps,
or have our eyes tested,
or go to a sit-down meal in a restaurant.
(A restaurant where one can typically see
couples, or entire families,
sitting in silence at a table
as they each gaze into smartphone screens;
often utilising the Internet of course).

It has displaced and replaced a great many things,
such as the art of mealtime conversation.

For some, the hypnotic scent of a bookshop still holds
much romance and magic.
The magnetism of music and movies is still with us,
but those are frequently accessed as digital files
on our machines, our devices.

We now have the choice of whether or not
to even enter a supermarket,
the entire list of all of the products in the store
is online.
Browse, add to the 'basket', click to pay,
and the deliveries magically come to our doors,
though usually harbouring unsatisfactory and
annoying substitutions.

Many of us still wish to walk around
and take some time and trouble
within the actual environment of stores,
but then some of us are still romantically nostalgic,
in a way that successive generations
may well not be.
Many high streets are full of empty,

110

deserted, derelict units.
Businesses that have been rendered unprofitable,
due to the competition from online retail providers
that have no unit rental overheads, nor staff to pay.
This phenomenon of new marauding market forces
that were traditionally so
revered by capitalist theorists,
has by no means claimed all of its
hapless victims yet.

The Web provides the complementary facility
for us to sell as well as to buy.
We are able to list any item that we wish to sell,
within minutes,
to a worldwide marketplace ourselves.
Billions of pounds changing hands every day.

We can create an online presence, an online
business
of our own.
Buy and sell things,
sell our own creations if we are skilled as
artists,
musicians,
writers,
perhaps web designers!

We can commission skilled web designers
or become skilled web designers.
We can construct our own websites,
to take whatever our desired content is
to the World, on this Wonderful World Wide Web.
There are also facilities to access,
for example, online tutorials.
Should we wish to change a car part,

learn to paint in acrylics,
set up a website,
or access any technical content for any reason,
somebody that knows
what we don't know,
but we want to know,
has been able to make their skills and knowledge
available for anybody that needs or wants them.

Just a click or two, as we sit in that armchair.

We can seek out and view educational content,
from academics and experts in
far-flung corners of the globe,
on any given topic or subject.
That magical click of a mouse
or swipe of a smartphone screen.

No longer do musicians have to prostrate themselves
before a god of judgement at a record company,
to release their music to their audiences.

No longer do poets and authors have to prostrate
themselves before gods of judgement
at publishing companies,
to release their work to their audiences.
Online dating, the chance to meet the one.
The Web, the Internet,
empowers people in profound ways,
and in these ways, it has transformed the world
and changed the lives of mankind and womankind.

Our children will grow up,
are growing up, with this technology
and will have completely different lives

112

than all previous generations have had.

The question that this begs, is,
better lives, or worse lives?
I am not going to even try and call that one.
It is too subjective to be answerable with logic alone.
We come to the double-edged sword
known as social media.

Both edges of the sword are
as sharp as razor blades.

When we first discover social media,
it comes across as the most beautiful enhancement
of our life and its scope.
All of a sudden, we find that we are able to connect.

New parameters of connection.
New depths of connection.
New breadths of connection.

We are able to find
long lost friends from our childhood,
from our schools,
and from our universities and colleges.

Family members, that we had given up hope
of ever seeing or hearing from,
suddenly we have new powers to trace.
Ex-boyfriends and ex-girlfriends,
whether they want to hear from us or not.
And then, connecting with people we have never met.
Like minds.
People with the same tastes in music,
or political leanings,

113

or followers of any particular cause,
people with similar spiritual groundings.
People that we just find we get along with.

'Friends'.

In many cases, people meet in a random context,
and end up as husband and wife,
where without the social media introduction
they would never have even known about
the existence of one another.
One's 'personal' page, one's 'business' page,
the sheer ease of finding people with whom
we have overlaps, commonality,
to whatever depths and breadths.
Visual images,
photographs of ourselves,
a further dimension of interaction,
possibly of attraction.

…….

And so now,
the other blade of that social media sword.

Membership of social media sites
requires the creation of a 'personal profile'.
Details of our background,
schools, higher education, employment.
Those photographs of ourselves,
perhaps of art we admire,
and so,
a picture of us as people.
Yet, we create it ourselves, and so
it can be a truth or a fabrication.
Love at first sight, but with a photograph

114

that is not a photograph of the person
whose page has a false name also.
How simple it is to manufacture deceit.

That ex-boyfriend, that ex-girlfriend,
the temptation to spy on them without them knowing.
Such subterfuge earns
the moniker of a 'lurker'.
And so, all of a sudden there
is a more sinister side to this
"beautiful enhancement of our life and its scope".
Most people are honest but some are not.
Most people have good intentions but some do not.
Most people are not sly,
calculating and Machiavellian,
but some are.
The empowerment empowers everyone,
whether they are good people or bad people.

A computer can copy a photograph in an instant,
and immediately a false identity and a false profile
are a piece of cake.

The only barrier to acquiring a new and
unique email address
is that somebody else has not already registered it.

And so an online dating profile, for example,
may have not a single shred of honest content.
A virtual person, by all meanings of 'virtual'.
A photograph of someone more attractive perhaps.
An invented education,
an invented amount of wealth,
an invented set of qualifications,
an invented occupation.

Everything to appear to be a better catch,
to receive more attention and interest,
from, ironically, perhaps a person that also doesn't
exist.

What an ideal playground for stalkers and predators.

People post photographs of themselves naked,
and ask others to do the same.

Adults pretend to be children or teenagers,
pretending to have things in common.
A video game, a band, a TV show,
a superhero or a film.
Sooner or later they may suggest to meet up.
The process has come to be referred to as
'grooming'.

Our images, our other data,
once uploaded to the Internet,
are almost impossible to delete permanently.

Everyone from, it seems,
toddler-age upwards,
has access to the Internet.
These interactions have given rise to some more of
Pandora's wares:
Mental health issues have risen exponentially.
Peer pressure has taken on a whole new dimension.

Cosmesis is booming, all the rage,
due to a pandemic of paranoia and insecurity.
Its sheer intensity,
an impossibility for some to cope with.
No young girl is anybody without big, puffy,

116

artificial lips full of filler,
because that is the route
to look just like everyone else,
and be accepted.
One assumes such things are worth the money,
but I, personally,
have yet to see anyone look better afterwards.
That's just my view.

I find it to be a deep well of widespread,
unquantifiable sadness.

Many have testified that
the acceptance itself is also artificial,
which they find after crossing that bridge;
in the same way that it said that wishing to be,
and then becoming, rich,
delivers no more happiness than that which
was already there beforehand.
Allegedly anyway, I wouldn't know.

The solutions to such troubling things,
such feelings and worries,
as anyone with any spirituality is aware,
are internal and not external.
Before having any hope of being accepted by others
must come the acceptance of oneself.
The reason that these epidemics are materialising,
is that the effects are influencing minds
that are simply not ready, not experienced enough
to process the complex nature of the pressures
involved.
And parents and loved ones have no idea of it
happening
until it has already happened,

117

and so the ability to solve, and to simply help,
is hampered and complicated
to much higher levels.
It is a double-edged sword,
but the tantalising lure of blade one,
and the apparent Utopia of ultimate connection,
that draws us all in like
a beautiful and powerful electromagnet,
has its hooks firmly into us
before the nightmarish ghoul of blade two
cuts down into our minds, our bodies and our souls.
For some, those cuts are deep and mortally
wounding,
which is why the mental health epidemic
has also been accompanied by
sharp spikes in the incidence of suicide.

…….

And so, without further ado:

The Pandora's Box inside the Pandora's Box…..

…… … …… …… …… …… …… …… …… …… …… …… …… …… ……

Pornography

Our miraculous Internet can bring 'content' to us
with the click of a mouse, or the tap of a trackpad,
or the touch of the screen of a smartphone.
It seems that everyone,
of almost any age,
has a smartphone.
Our kids are in touch if they get lost
or are in some kind of trouble.
Smartphones are everybody's best friend.

The access to almost every piece of information,
or works in any of the world's libraries,
is indeed a technological miracle.
But it takes just the same one or two steps
to access a pornographic website.
All that's needed is to click 'Yes'
when it asks if you are 18.
I am about to speak of almost unspeakable things,
but I will cheat just a little bit
by not explaining meanings within the terminology.
I will use terms that people either already know,
can work out just by reading the words,
or can easily search for on that Wonderful Web.

I have not, nor any wish to have,
either experience or knowledge of
accessible content which is illegal,
but let me make a promise,
that which is legal is more than sufficient
to have the effects I will issue grave warnings about.
At least that is my humble opinion,
but as ever, grounded in solid logic and fact.
All a hormonal teenage boy needs, remember,
is one or two clicks, and teenage boys
love to share such information as website titles
when the content is as I will now outline.
And even if word of mouth does not name websites,
everybody knows how to use an
Internet search engine.

'Conventional sex',
that where the male and female organs
obey the biology
of what they are 'supposed to do',
is a natural process, that would commonly occur

119

in the bedrooms of adults, within safe situations.
It is sometimes described as 'vaginal sex'.
Vaginal penetration and ejaculation,
although often the ejaculation is seen
outside of the vagina
and instead onto the faces, or other body parts,
of the participating actors or actresses.

For the uninitiated, blissfully oblivious parent,
I am referring to
100% graphic camera angles, nothing hidden.
Numerous sexual positions abound,
one could almost regard it as educational.
Ideas, perhaps, for a varied sex life.
Harmless enough?
Natural, and many permutations of 'how to'.

'Oral sex', either way,
so either 'cunnilingus' or 'fellatio'.
Something else that one imagines happens
between most couples.
Yet even as I refer to
these more 'normal', natural contexts
to viewable pornography,
in general these are adult pursuits,
carried out by adults,
learned about by minds that are able
and mature enough
to process them.

'Anal sex' scenes
are as readily visible as the conventional ones.
Scenes from Italian pornography
almost always contain
anal penetration.

120

In my opinion
the prevalence of this material
would impress a young teenage boy
as being as acceptable,
as commonplace, and as 'normal',
as vaginal penetration.
It is as visible to a mind that is ready,
mature and able to process it,
as it is to a mind that is not.

Without any relevant experience.
Without enough information to contextualise it at all.

I politely suggest
that a hormonal teenage boy
would be unlikely to discuss such matters
with their parents.
I would suggest that
hormonal teenage boys
would not even consider that there was even
anything to ask about, or discuss,
with anybody,
because the inability to process it,
the very dangerous problem itself,
the boys are not conscious of.
The very prevalence of the material
would cause the deduction of its
normality and acceptability.
Of course females access pornography too,
but the vast majority of consumers
are known to be male
and I am making my point about
young males specifically.

And this is not just simply my opinion,

logical though my opinion is.

Apparently, family doctors are being visited
by increasing numbers of teenage girls.
Teenage girls with rectal injuries and internal injuries.
Girls that have had to try and explain to their parents
how such injuries came about.
Boyfriends that thought that
anal sex was acceptable and normal.
On the evidence they had observed, it is.

Anal sex scenes are portrayed as
enjoyable and painless.
It is rare that any depiction or suggestion
of artificial lubrication is present.

A member of my own family was anally raped
at the age of 15, by her boyfriend,
in the safety of his parents' home,
in the safety of his bedroom.

A teenage boy will not question or
understand such details,
but he can access the pornography
at any time he wants.
Where, who, are the boundaries,
the limits, the yardstick,
going to come from?
And pornography,
due to the biochemistry of arousal and
orgasm, is intensely addictive.
It is no exaggeration to refer to it as a powerful DRUG.
A drug, though, that is free of charge at many sites.
Only an Internet connection is required.

Outside of heinous,
notorious aberrations and exceptions,
in an adult
that addiction is not necessarily a dangerous one
as long as the adult is able to
process and contextualise it.

There is much more content that most younger
teenagers, in my estimation,
are not generally ready to witness:

Double penetration.
Double vaginal intercourse.
Double anal intercourse.
Fisting.
Golden showers.
BDSM.
Bukkake.
Gangbangs.
Group sex, orgies.
Two women, one man.
Two men, one woman.
Scenes with geriatric performers,
men and women,
with much younger performers.
Incest storylines of all imaginable permutations.
Participants of all shapes and sizes,
(which means body sizes and/or organ sizes).
Solo masturbation, both male and female.
Masturbation of someone else, perhaps
simultaneous mutual masturbation
between participants.
Homosexual scenes as well as heterosexual scenes,
applying all the same permutations
as already mentioned.

Women having choke holds to the throat during sex.
Spoofs of actual movies, with tacky tweaked titles.
Full length movies.
Scenes from many other countries around the world.
Pornography is indeed worldwide,
because wherever there is the Internet, there it is.

Numerous different settings are staged:

A schoolroom
(rest assured that content on legal websites
will only have adult participants,
but it clearly plants specific thoughts).
A next door neighbour's house.
Outdoors, in public or private places.
A hospital.
A stately home.
A peeping tom.
A night club.
A dungeon.
Romantic, more emotional scenes, uncommonly.
Burglaries.
Intruders.
Simulated rape.
More conventional consenting surprise scenes.
Dildos.
Vibrators.
Butt-plugs.
Double-ended dildos for 2 women.

'Sounding' devices.

Costumes:
Nurses.
Doctors.

124

Policemen and women.
Maids, in houses or hotels.
Superheroes.
Witches.
Prison officers.
Latex garments of all types.
PVC.
Masks.
Cages.
Many other 'role-playing' simulations.

Thousands upon thousands of scenes
on just some single sites.
Click, after click, after click, after click, after click.

Personally, I am quite squeamish
with regard to 'porn',
and I find that much of the content,
though perfectly legal, to me is unnatural,
and is often too abusive and disrespectful to women.
If I feel that way about it, at my age,
I do fear of the effects on the boys,
them still being boys.
I call this sub-piece 'Pandora's Box',
because when these images have been seen,
they cannot be unseen.
I fear that this is a phenomenon, a time bomb,
just like the explosion in mental health problems,
which we are yet to see the real extent of.
I fear for the youngsters,
the boys and the girls,
who do not make informed choices
about such things before they witness them.

Witnessing them is initially

an accidental occurrence
out of normal, natural, innocent curiosity,
like Pandora opening her box.

I fear that the snowballs are already rolling
down a steep slope, to who knows where.
Snowballs of misunderstood sexuality,
resulting in multiplication and escalation
of bad outcomes, precipitated by
unhealthy, unbalanced
and maladjusted minds,
thanks to that exposure to all
that inappropriately potent material,
without the correct, or any,
context within the mind of the recipient.
The consumer.

Every parent, of every son and daughter
should know about this.
This is not written for my recreation.

My knowledge is going to be
more limited than some,
and less limited than some.
My son is an adult.
My stepdaughters are adults.

But if they were all much younger
and I were ignorant of these matters,
I would read this and be grateful
that somebody had written it down,
as it would be a safe way of finding out
compared to far worse possible ways.

The Internet is both a blessing and a curse,

but it has effects that are irreversible,
though myself, I refuse to be saturnine.

I like to believe that
Hope
is still there
in Pandora's box.

Professionalism Personified

I am not a big fan of the Royal Family,
not in theory, nor in principle, nor in practice,
because I do not believe in inequality
on the basis of parameters,
and factors,
that make absolutely no sense.
I think I have made that sentiment very clear already.

However, if we place the obscene,
illogical elitism to one side,
the Royal Family are human beings.
And I do believe in respect between human beings.

I also believe
that it is totally fair and reasonable
to call out people that do not
respect the principle
of respecting people.

I would like to begin my appraisal
by listing the names of some people
that I feel like calling out in such a manner:

(alphabetically by publication)

The editor of Cosmo, Michele Promaulayko.
The editor of Country Living, Susy Smith.
The editor of the Daily Express, Gary Jones.
The editor of the Daily Mirror, Lloyd Embley.
The editor of Elle, Nina Garcia.
The editor of the Evening Standard, George Osborne.
The editor of Good Housekeeping, Jane Francisco.

The editor of Hello! magazine, Rosie Nixon.
The editor of Instyle, Laura Brown.
The editor of Marie Claire, Trish Halpin.
The editor of OK magazine, Kirsty Tyler.
The editor of People magazine, Jess Cagle.
The editor of The Sun, Tony Gallagher.
The editor of Town & Country, Stellene Volandes.

Journalists, some of whom sport the title
of Royal Correspondent, but since
that title makes no difference to my assertions,
and makes any mistakes I may make more likely,
I will not add that irrelevant layer of information:

(alphabetically by publication and surname)

Dusty Baxter-Wright (Cosmo).
Mehera Bonner (Cosmo, Good Housekeeping).
Sophie Boyden (Cosmo).
Laura Capon (Cosmo).
Jess Edwards (Cosmo).
Erica Gonzalez (Cosmo, Harper's Bazaar).
Alanna Lauren Greco (Cosmo).
Catriona Harvey-Jenner (Cosmo).
Amy Mackelden (Country Living).
Richard Palmer (Daily Express).
Camilla Tominey (Daily Express).
Rebecca English (Daily Mail).
Victoria Murphy (Daily Mirror).
Nicola Oakley (Daily Mirror).
Alyssa Bailey (Elle).
Holly Rhue (Elle).
Hatty Collier (Evening Standard).
Emily Nash (Hello!).
Hollie Richardson (Hello!).

129

Alexandra Whittaker (Instyle).
Carly Ledbetter (HuffPost)
Penny Goldstone (Marie Claire).
Jenny Proudfoot (Marie Claire).
Kayleigh Roberts (Marie Claire).
Jadie Troy-Pryde (Marie Claire).
Lucy Wood (Marie Claire).
Joanna Freedman (OK).
Monique Jessen (People).
Maria Pasquini (People).
Stephanie Petit (People).
Emily Andrews (The Sun).
Caroline Hallemann (Town & Country).
Maggie Maloney (Town & Country).
Sarah Carty (Yahoo Style UK).
Rebekah Scanlan (Yahoo Style UK).
Francesca Specter (Yahoo Style UK).

I do not have anything like the level of interest
in expanding this list of people
to go to the 'nth degree' of research,
just to produce a longer list
for the sheer sake of doing so.
This will not certainly not be
an exhaustive list of culprits.

I would bet my entire collection of gold bullion,
that a nice chap named Hugo Double-Barrel
advised me to buy
when he called me out of the blue one morning,
which I keep safely under my bed,
camouflaged with a blanket,
that this list could easily be 50 times as long.
The gold bullion is doing really well though,
Hugo said,

so a bet of such magnitude
shows my confidence in saying so.

My general impression
of editors and journalists
is a little cynical.
I am not sure though,
what a stressful burden it must be
to write columns about
the talented Kardashian sisters,
or the 'A list' cast of
The Only Way Is Essex,
or which designers' dresses
everybody wore to the awards ceremony,
or the topic I am involved in here.
As for editors, I assume they have to convey
their owners' narratives and agendas
without making it
patently obvious that they are doing that.

I don't believe they succeed in doing it
nearly as much as they would like to think.
Perhaps gullibility is widespread
and perhaps it is not.

I digress.

I hope that the degrees in journalism,
that people work so hard for,
have prepared them well to make their content
in general matters like and unlike this one,
better than the created impression
I will now open up about.

Kate Middleton,
on 29th April 2011,
at Westminster Abbey,
got married to the heir to the throne,
Prince William,
and they became the
Duke and Duchess of Cambridge.

Meghan Markle,
on 19th May 2018,
at Windsor Castle,
got married to Prince Harry,
William's younger brother,
sixth in line to the throne,
and they became the
Duke and Duchess of Sussex.

Every single
editor and journalist
I have mentioned
has participated or approved,
many of them a great many times,
in referring in headlines,
as well as within articles in many cases,
to the Duchess of Cambridge
as 'Kate Middleton',
in fact they are still doing it in 2019,
eight years after the marriage.
I have not yet seen headline
nor content
about 'William Windsor', ever.
I am told he signs his name as
William Cambridge
which may or may not be true,
but I haven't seen that name in print either.

Every single
editor and journalist listed
has participated or approved,
many of them a great many times,
in referring in headlines,
as well as within articles in many cases,
to the Duchess of Sussex
as 'Meghan Markle',
and I expect will continue to do so
for at least the next seven years.
I have not yet seen
headline nor content
about 'Harry Windsor', ever.
I am told he signs his name as
Harry Sussex
which may or may not be true,
but I haven't seen that name in print either.
I get the feeling that accuracy is entirely worthless to
various people within the printed media.

There is a term used
for much online 'journalism' content nowadays
and it is completely self-explanatory.

Clickbait.

The dizzy heights of journalistic endeavour.

I would not be in the least surprised
if the offices of publications
resemble old-fashioned direct sales offices,
where staff have targets
for numbers of clicks they generate
and records of click numbers to try and smash.
That is, however,

133

just my educated guess and suspicion.

....

So, to be completely clear,
Princes William and Harry are given respect
whilst the Duchesses are treated like
lumps of crap.
I thought equality between the sexes
was revered and observed
in our so-called United Kingdom.
What a joke.

Though we are very familiar with some
editors and journalists
doing whatever the hell they want,
regardless of what is right or wrong.
Even the Royal couples' children
are referred to by their charming,
though admittedly highly pretentious, titles.

--.--

Interestingly,
most of the journalists,
and some of the editors,
are women.
I happen to know,
from doing a little more
research than I probably
should have bothered with, merit-wise,
that some of these named women are married.
So I would like to ask some open questions to them.

Unless you are a trendy, hypocritical feminist type
(I say 'hypocritical' with specific reference
to the treatment of the Royals)

134

that has chosen to continue
to use your maiden name,
how would you feel
if either your friends, your acquaintances,
or people that don't know you whatsoever
decided to call you, repeatedly, disrespectfully,
by your maiden name?

Do you call your own married friends,
or acquaintances,
family members,
or people that you don't know at all,
(such as the Duchesses of Cambridge and Sussex)
by their maiden names?
How is it appropriate to address
the Princes as Prince William and Prince Harry,
or the Dukes of Cambridge and Sussex,
in completely different ways
to their chosen lifelong partners
that now also have equally legitimate titles?

This question is multiple choice.

There are only two options.
It's 50-50.
Surely everybody can get this one right?
It's even easier than The Chase
where you have to choose one from three.
Is this behaviour:

A: Acceptable?
B: Disrespectful, inaccurate, inappropriate,
unprofessional, ignorant, and downright rude?

The Press, of course,

135

are generally a law unto themselves.
They often love to attack scapegoats,
they often love to exercise shamefully obvious bias.
They often love to manipulate and lie
and use the various well-worn tools of Propaganda,
so this whole matter is simply
no more than typical behaviour.

I accept, and have noticed,
that sometimes, within the pieces
that these honourable lady journalists write,
they refer to the Duchesses by their titles.
Even sometimes,
though much more rarely,
within the headlines too.
But their husbands are always referred to
by their Prince, or Duke, titles.
Always.
100% of the time.

I had a curious browse through

Marie Claire magazine in a shop,
and of the 175 or so pages, about 170 of them
appeared to be just advertisements.
What a snip at £4.20.
It prompts the question,
regardless of the subjects being royalty
as it applies equally to any subject of any article,
who do these people think they are?

But then,
I have been asking that question about
journalists and editors
since shortly after mastering

the reading of newspapers
at the age of three years old.
I know who I think they are in a great many cases.
It rhymes with hunts. As in Jeremy.

Did I say that my impression of
editors and journalists
is a little cynical?

Is there any middle ground
between the trashy, boring,
celebrity gossip, clickbait output
and the shameless,
transparent-to-most Propaganda
outside of broadsheets?

…·…

Are people with
hard-earned degrees in journalism
proud of what they do
with their educated, qualified time?

Are they simply paid
such obscene amounts of money
that they just close their eyes,
lie back and think of
the so-called United Kingdom?

I repeat:
I am not a fan of the Royal Family,
just a believer in respect between human beings,
and I feel it is fair
when people overstep the mark
and treat anyone, even royalty, like crap,
to call them out.

I like editors and journalists,
on the whole,
not just less than the Royal Family,
but less than pretty much any group of people
with the exception of certain breeds of politician,
and maybe the mountebanks that cold-call people
to persuade them to part with their money.

Although, my friend Hugo Double-Barrel
does sound like a
well-educated, intelligent man
with a very posh voice,
and I would trust him with my life.

Of course,
my green envious face
cannot be camouflaged,
I myself can only
dream of being paid to
write worthless, inconsequential dross.

It won't happen.

It can't.

I don't have a degree in journalism.

And I do have a modicum of pride.

The Rabies of Propaganda

You're a what? A Muslim?
How dare you build a mosque in this
so-called United Kingdom!
'United' does not include
You Lot.
We couldn't build a church in
one of 'your' countries,
after all.

Despite the fact
that the only time
the British ever go to church
is for pretty wedding photos.
But the truth doesn't fit the story,
so you'll get the story and not the truth.

You don't integrate!
You speak three languages?
Oh. Sorry. I didn't realise.
No, of course I wouldn't learn
a foreign language
if I emigrated,
I'm British.
People have to speak my language.
But the truth doesn't fit the story,
so you'll get the story and not the truth.

Do not use the word refugees,
it implies that migrants are
actual human beings.
It gives the wrong impression,
the impression that they should be respected.

Anyway we just don't have room
for any more people here.

The 33% of ex-pats planning to return here,
You can't. Sorry.
Britain is full,
didn't you hear it on the news?

When I look out of the windows of trains
I see nothing but expanses of open space,
but it seems there's none spare for foreigners.
Our hospitals are too full
with smokers, the obese
and drunks who have been fighting,
and irresponsible drunk drivers,
and their victims,
to treat any foreign children or elderly.
But the truth doesn't fit the story,
so you'll get the story and not the truth.

The EU is a bureaucracy of unelected dictators!
Though it is a fact that the EU Commission,
which is unelected,
has no powers to pass legislation.
Only the elected representatives
of the EU Parliament
have the power to pass laws.
Does Nigel 'Foxhunter' Farage know?
You bet he does,
he's been a member of that Parliament
for 20-odd years.

So why doesn't he tell his blind supporters?
There's a question, blind supporters,
to ask the dishonourable chap.

A question that I think anyone can answer.
He can't hide from his initials being 'NF'

Does Boris (The Hairbrush) Johnson know?
Oh yes, you bet he does.
He is, I am told,
a clever man,
(he studied at Eton and Oxford, remember),
that puts on an ACT of being
a cumbersome buffoon, it's not real.
So why doesn't he tell his gullible followers?
There's a question, gullible followers,
another question that I think anyone can answer.
Are facts simply not relevant because it's politics?
Is this exactly how all this is supposed to work?
The truth doesn't fit the story,
so you'll get the story and not the truth.

What makes anyone think that
old Jacob Rees-Mogg,
that I have said plenty about already,
he and his fruitcake mind
that were born 300 years too late,
yet another Oxford Alumnus,
after Margaret Thatcher,
and Tony Blair,
and David Cameron,
and George Osborne,
and Theresa May,
and Jeremy Hunt,
and Boris Johnson,

is likely to help anybody that actually needs help?
Rather than helping those that don't need help?
But the owners of tabloids are rich.

141

So as the truth doesn't fit the story,
you'll get the story and not the truth.

Nigel Farage, in contrast, didn't attend a university.
Hearing his pompous shouts of disrespect
in the European Parliament,
aimed at many individuals cleverer than himself,
suggests he has chips,
or maybe whole Maris Piper potatoes,
on both shoulders.
Why is he always shouting at everybody?

He will surely burst a blood vessel,
he should calm down a bit.
He's on a cushy, lucrative Gravy Train mind you.
He seems terribly ungrateful
and hypocritical
I must say.
I doubt I'm alone in thinking that.
I'm absolutely certain that I'm not.
Especially if I canvassed that chamber.

He thinks that the 51.89% Brexit vote
should be honoured
as the democratic will of the people, yet
the estimated 84% of Britons
that wish fox hunting
to "remain" illegal,
should not be obeyed,
because they are
interfering with other people's lives.

Is he a hypocrite, or just an imbecile? Both?
I think that a scientist,
or perhaps a mathematician

should give him a little assistance, to
help him understand
that 84 is a larger number than 51.89.
The poor chap seems to have a
mental block with numbers as big as 84.

Nigel Farage has tried to become an MP
but couldn't pull it off.
Perhaps then, it's not surprising
that he finds it very difficult
to deal with the likes of
Guy Verhofstadt,
the ex-Prime Minister of Belgium,
or Donald Tusk,
the ex-Prime Minister of Poland.
It seems a lot more likely though,
that it is they that find it difficult to deal with him,
perhaps when trying to explain things to him
that are beyond his intellectual grasp.
Those Maris Pipers will be very heavy by now.

We should have a pity whipround
and buy him some books and a calculator,
or at least an abacus.

..—..

Brexit in a nutshell:

the House Of Commons is elected
but members of the Cabinet are appointed.
And so the ministers with any power are
not elected
to their posts.
The House Of Lords is not elected.
Permanent Secretaries are not elected.

143

The monarchy is not elected.
The EU Commission is not elected
but has no power.
The EU Parliament is elected
and has the power.
Please stop me if I'm going too fast.

It would be nice if a Brexit-supporting liar
would clear all of that up
for the poor, gullible blind,
but the truth doesn't fit the story,
so you'll get the story and not the truth.

Did you read this morning's Daily _____?
The tabloid 'news'papers have all sorts of
strategies, approaches and techniques.
Quite sneaky intentions,
but ever so easy to spot, fortunately.
To indulge in Propaganda one needs the tools,
but without sufficient subtlety it falls flat on its face.
I'm not sure that they're aware
when they make things too obvious though.

Not just what is said, but what is not said.
Complete omission of important content.
Often the most important parts are,
in fact, the withheld ones.

There is Misinformation - that is just lies,
fake news, to you or me.
Often they don't pull that one off very well either.

Character Assassination, sometimes called
scapegoating,
or persecution,

or a witch hunt,
the purpose of which is
to discredit a person's reputation
and to smear their good name.
That is also par for the course in
certain vehicles of Propaganda.

For example,
let's say I annoy somebody.
Unlikely, but possible, I'm mostly nice.
I left Oxford University after 2 years.
My course, unusually,
was 4 years and not 3, and I left,
which I decided after weighing up
a number of options that I was offered.
An article appears.
It is meant to catch me by surprise
and discredit and embarrass me.
The Daily _____ calls me a drop-out,
didn't make the grade. Stupid, therefore.
'Stu Pid'.
I go by it on social media now & then.
The funny thing is,
the journalist and the editor in question
both applied to Oxford University
to do PPE, and were rejected.
Plus, they don't get the full background story and so I
get the opportunity to turn the tables.
I don't bother to,
because it's a silly, trivial battle
that I don't care about.

My schizophrenia,
and the criminal record that it gave rise to,
are another couple of skeletons in my cupboards.

145

A severe and incurable mental illness can show you
the darkest places in the universe -
but don't expect compassion from a gutter tabloid
if they don't like you.
Expect instead
to feel a knife in your back,
and then to feel it being twisted.

Anybody, for any reason, is a legitimate target.

Take Jeremy Corbyn.
If you support the Palestinian cause
you are an anti-Semite?

The Labour Party gets accused
of being riddled with anti-Semitism.
The rampant Islamophobic racism
among the Conservatives is
mysteriously absent from all media outlets,
written and broadcast.
The trouble is that everyone is Internet-savvy,
and all the Propaganda fails,
because people have Googled the truth elsewhere.

Take Russell Brand.

A silly prank, or, say, a radical viewpoint.
Spiteful journalists go literally crazy
with absolute, jealous rubbish.
They can't write enough
inconsequential dross about him.
'Inconsequential dross' is my pet name
for inconsequential dross.
Russell is smarter,
and a professional comedian,

and so goes onto the Internet,
and ruthlessly and effortlessly takes the piss,
and makes it clear to the Daily _____ that
he couldn't care less.
If the truth doesn't fit the story
you'll get the story and not the truth.

But it's so, so, so,
patently obvious most of the time,
and the readership of Propaganda are
70+ years old,
and there's only 42 of them alive now anyway.
The key word here is 'obsolete'.

Germany.
We hate them, they were our sworn enemies.
There were some very nasty people there,
but it was generations ago.
We have to hate them now
because we are leaving the EU.

We hate them because they have
a healthier economy than ours.

We hate Angela Merkel,

she has too much influence,
though she has been democratically elected
for the 4th time.

Excuse me while I pick up my shiny new BMW.
The new and brilliant Mercedes-Benz range.
The fabulous design of the new Audi.
The iconic Volkswagen Beetle convertible.
The BMW Mini, that was saved from British failure.

A Porsche Cayenne, maybe a Panamera or 911?
I cannot wait to buy a new German car.
My Bosch dishwasher
and Blaupunkt car stereo
are so reliable.

But I hate Germany and the Germans,
because I belong in the past,
in a previous generation.

On the subject of Germans;
in 1917,
the British Royal Family changed its name
from Saxe-Coburg-Gotha to Windsor.
It sounds a lot more British,
and less embarrassing,
especially as 'we' were
fighting against Germany at the time.
So that is Queen Elizabeth's side, and then;
Prince Philip was born Philippos Andreou of
Schleswig-Holstein-Sonderberg-Glucksburg,
Prince of Greece and Denmark.
Not a lot of tabloid readers
and one-dimensional thinkers
are aware of such things,
because the truth doesn't fit the story,
so we are given the story and not the truth.

‑‑·‑‑

Pope Francis said very publicly,
in a speech in Ireland in the summer of 2018,
how ashamed he was of the paedophilia
within the Catholic Church.
Noble words. Though, in themselves, only words.
Am I the only one noticing the silence?

The absence of resignations and excommunications?
Does the rhetoric simply
serve to make clear
that the culture of secrecy
and protection of evil acts,
and their perpetrators, continues?
Was the expectation
that this Pope was genuine,
different, progressive even,
another exercise in manipulation
of the hopes of honest people?

Was it simply another example
of a story instead of the truth?
On my car radio, in icy December,
a news item announced
that Pope Francis had asked any church officials
that had committed acts
of paedophilia in the past,
or perhaps indulge
in paedophilia in the present,
to come forward.
I suggest,
with the utmost respect,
that a polite request,
to a child molester,
to 'come forward',
and destroy his own reputation,
and remove his own livelihood,
and display his evil and abhorrent
secrets to the world,
and effectively,
to all intents and purposes,
end most aspects of his life,
and bring about a situation

where nobody that he knows trusts him,
and nobody he ever will know will trust him

IS NOT EXACTLY THE SAME AS

IS NOT REMOTELY THE SAME AS

IS NOTHING LIKE THE SAME AS

throwing out every single known paedophile.
All of them.
Finding, and throwing out,
every as yet unknown paedophile.
All of them.

Going through church and Vatican records,
those top-secret files that
nobody gets to look at.

I wonder why it is that
nobody gets to look at them.
Unless there are ugly things to hide,
why the secrecy?

But what a fabulous, perfect Utopia, what a
paradise!
The end of all ills in our world!

Oyez, oyez, oyez!
Oyez, oyez, oyez!
Oyez, oyez, oyez!

Could all of you that have burgled houses,
all of you that have injured someone,
or killed someone,

150

exceeded the speed limit in a motor vehicle,
dropped litter in a park,
stolen money or belongings from somebody,
committed fraud or deception,
or, obviously,
touched - and abused - and defiled
the innocent body of an innocent child
while in a position of trust,
that one goes without saying
because it is so......

DIABOLICAL
in the literal meaning of the word,
'of the Devil',

please declare your crimes
and all related or unrelated
dark secrets.

Then please go to the prison,
lock yourself into a cell,
and stay there for a period of 10 years.
Thank you.

Crime is rendered optional
when admitting to it is made optional,
Commit any crimes you wish
and either tell us
or not tell us
about it.
......

Let's see, another piece of lunacy.
When Boris Johnson was appointed
as Foreign Secretary,
it was a perfect example of something called

'high irony'.
In other words,
a man that has insulted many countries,
(despite countries being insentient blobs of land),
the people of many countries and
the officials of many countries,
was appointed to spearhead
our international relations.
So, a contradiction in terms.
Was Theresa May serious
or playing a huge practical joke?
It is frequently difficult to tell.

The only higher irony that I can bring to mind
was the appointment of Tony Blair as
'Middle East Peace Envoy',
while the bodies of the dead
were still on the desert sand,
and their blood was barely dry.

No Weapons of Mass Destruction,
of course, were ever found.
But the truth didn't fit the story
and the secret plans.
So we got the story and not the truth,
and, of course, as a bonus, a war.

......

There are documents locked away
under 'secrecy legislation'
for many different lengths of time.
Usually when this is invoked, the words
'National Security'
are centre stage.
We are all in mortal danger
if such information were to be public.

152

Or perhaps, just perhaps,
instead of any threat
whatsoever to the nation,
once in a while,
allegedly, somebody's reputation
would be damaged.

The more so-called 'senior' the person,
the more the
absolute necessity
they be protected.
A Cabinet minister.
A Prime Minister.
A Royal Family member.
You get the idea.

Have a look at the files,
opened after 30 years, no less,
referring to Margaret 'Baroness' Thatcher's
despicable lies,
and strategies, and methods,
during the miners' strike.

Smears of Arthur Scargill's character,
when it was she that was
doing the sinister plotting, all along.
Even her 'adversary' Neil Kinnock helped out.
The story, not the truth.

Those documents were buried
for that one reason.
She had them buried purely to
protect her own reputation.
Seeing her tears

153

when unceremoniously kicked out of
10 Downing Street by her own party, and
Sir Geoffrey Howe's beautiful
'stab-in-the-back' speech,
were just priceless
as well as completely justified.
I will very soon be saying much more about
Margaret Hilda Thatcher.

Watch the film 'The Bank Job',
based on true events no less,
which they had to wait
30 years
to even be able to make.
See how people were tortured,
and murdered,
by British officials,
not all that long ago at all,
purely to protect
Princess Margaret's skin
after her sexual indiscretions.

Some of those documents
are still buried until 2054.
That's a long time.

Postponing content for so long
removes, of course,
all accountability.
The dead cannot be shamed or prosecuted.
There may be inaccuracies in the film,
but I am only talking of principles,
and I am also in the dark,
obviously, like everyone else,
with regard to exactly

154

what is hidden in such secret files.

One thing I do know is this;
whenever I hear the words
'National Security',
I am certain I am about to be lied to,
and something covered up.

A flagrant example from
no earlier than the end of 2017,
with reference to child abuse allegations
against Cyril Smith
(awarded a knighthood
by Margaret 'Baroness' Thatcher in 1988),
Theresa May and Amber Rudd
saw fit to withhold documents
pertaining to the investigation.

The documents, allegedly,
were a "threat to our National Security".

A child abuse probe,
into a seemingly odious
and long dead man,
allegedly,
needed to be hidden in order
to protect the country's safety?
It seems we, the British people,
were all born yesterday.

Is this rocket science,
brain surgery,
theoretical physics?
My long shot at reading between the lines
is that one or more names,

155

connected with some
incriminating and embarrassing content,
are being withheld to protect someone's
High Society Arse.

It did not seem to attract
the attention of the media, either,
oddly. How odd!

The putrifying stench in this case is that of the
corpse of accountability,
rotting ever more overpoweringly
in the rancid tomb
where secrets, lies and cover-ups
are locked away,
piled up by, and for, Establishment figures.
I expect that it is just a freakish coincidence
that no investigation into
high-level and organised
child abuse
ever even gets off the ground.
Who knows what is kept from us.

Editors and journalists are
not interested in that one either.
They would rather emblazon their front pages
with stories like
Jeremy Corbyn kicking a
pensioner's defenceless small dog to death,
treading on the cracks in the pavement, or
shaking hands with a person of ethnic origin, or
having an offensive arrangement of his facial hair, or
buying a bicycle from the wrong shop.
Distractions, Distractions, Distractions.

Propaganda, Propaganda, Propaganda.

If the truth doesn't fit the story,
we'll be getting the story instead of the truth.
As always.

It's just so, so, so, boring.

I really have no idea
who they think is affected or convinced.
An insult to the intelligence of
those last 42 paying septuagenarian readers
and nobody gives a fucking sparrow's shit.

.....

A brief word about the public narratives of Brexit.
I read the ballot paper,
it gave me an unambiguous, simple choice;

Remain in the European Union or
Leave the European Union.
No more, no less.
How much more simple could it be?
Many people say, incorrectly,
that some detail was somehow there too.

"Walk away, no deal.
That's what we voted for."
"The Irish border? Stays as it is.
That's what we voted for."
"No immigrants, unless you're a doctor.
It's what we voted for."
"Out of the Single Market.
Trade with the whole world."
"Out of the Customs Union. We don't need them."

157

"The EU are unelected dictators. Take our country back."
"Take back control of our laws."

How about this instead, something I read,
shorter and so much sweeter;

"Let's make Britain great again -
kick out all the racists."

Austerity.

Reduce the budgets for all departments, every year.

Less police, never mind that we are less safe as a result.

Less doctors and nurses, that's alright,
just make them all work even more.

Less money for those on benefits.
Disqualify higher numbers from getting any benefits.
Blame immigrants for everything, say that it's they
that are squeezing the services.
Bollocks.

Less money for education - just privatise. Academies.

Less money for councils – empty the bins half as often.

Tell everybody it's necessary.
Tell everybody it's all about inefficiency,
things need 'streamlining'.
Tell them it's sensible economics and accounting.

158

Pretend that doing all this improves the economy
When it does nothing of the sort.
I'll be explaining it properly.

Meanwhile, whispers, behind closed doors;
"the public are too stupid to understand such things.

The Far-Right media will play ball with us,
and with their Propaganda,
the 42 readers will be convinced of these lies."

The _story_ and not the _truth_
are what is made relevant,
in order to continue to
control, distract and _manipulate_ the people
that the _government_ are supposed to _serve_.
And _everything_ we _see_ and _hear_
has come through a _filtration system_ of _censorship_.

That's Propaganda in action.

A final, clear example:
I have lost count of the number of times,
on television news programmes,
be they on Sky,
or the famously impartial BBC,
or ITV,
when an issue is being 'discussed',
we are introduced to two 'experts'.
You would ignorantly, logically, objectively think
that there would be an 'expert' providing
each side of the issue.
How naive to think such a thing.

No, no, no.

159

All expectations of balanced output
are soon dismissed.
It's actually just two
slightly different types of 'expert',
both on the same side of the issue in question.

As I said, I have completely lost count.

The cumulative effects of the Propaganda
are as violent,
and dangerous,
and easy to catch,
as a bout of rabies
from the foaming mouth of a mad dog.
One that bites you
a number of times,
every single day.

Question everything.

You are wasting your time and money
if you are obtaining your news,
your information,
your Propaganda,
your narratives,
your storylines,
your fairy tales,
your Propaganda,
your lies,
your half-truths,
your doses of The Rabies Of Propaganda
from the same sources
and, or, the wrong sources.
Use your insight and your judgement.

Most ideally, we all should
seek out and learn how to open our Third Eye.

We possess the instinct to see through deception,
it only needs to be activated.

Strategic Styles

There is a lot of mileage and relevance in analysing some of the strategies and tactics which different Prime Ministers have used over the years. In a few cases they are very simple to pick apart, and see what sort of 'mirror image' it gives of the values and attributes (I doubt you will have any problem deciding what positive and/or negative traits you observe) of the individuals. I will not be analysing John Major or Gordon Brown, because 1) they did not attend an Oxford college, that is actually relevant as will reveal itself, and I am in part observing a trend, 2) they did not employ such overt policies, and 3) in both cases, they had far too much humanity in their hearts to be placed amongst those that I shall include.

So, in alphabetical order by surname:

<u>Blair, Tony. (Prime Minister 1997 - 2007)</u>

Tony Blair got his opportunity to occupy 10 Downing Street due to the untimely death of the very popular and respected John Smith on the 12th May 1994. We did not see enough of Mr. Smith's leadership to build much of a detailed picture, but I feel confident in saying that Tony Blair's style was very different to Mr. Smith's.

Tony Blair was a cool guy, a hip guy, I mean he was in a band at one point for goodness' sake. His beaming smile was one of his trademarks, along with his bedside manner - if the sun was out and you were unlucky enough to catch a reflection of the rays off Tony's gleaming gnashers, you'd be lucky to keep your

162

eyesight intact. And that, quite seamlessly, leads into the real subject matter regarding Tony's strategy which won him three General Elections. Just like the temporary blindness from the reflection off his teeth, the approach that he and his arch-cronies Peter Mandelson and Alastair Campbell took to the people was to put together an advertising campaign. A slick marketing and re-branding of the whole Labour Party itself. Tony's unwavering crescent of shining white choppers at the forefront.

Labour became New Labour. Astounding. It must have taken a team of five history graduates a whole week to come up with it, a stroke of genius. But it was snappy, it was repeated hundreds of times in the voters' ears as all the best slogans are, and it was pretty damned true - because New Labour was a completely different political machine than traditional Old Labour. It could barely be more different. It was not about ideology at all, it was just about winning, and putting together a strategy to achieve it. He was aiming to get away with murder, though at this early stage, not literally. And ideally without anybody noticing.

(It is so ironic, and not for the last time within the story of Tony Blair, that he was the only recent Oxford Alumnus Prime Minister that studied Law. Keep that in mind).

When Tony Blair was elected Prime Minister, he gave a speech about remembering that it was he that worked for the British people, and not the other way round. But then, it was only his first day. He hadn't learned the proper skill set at that point. Or perhaps he was beginning to deliberately mislead everyone already.

Bearing in mind the overt marketing and branding element of the way New Labour was promoted, it wasn't long, and it had been inevitable, that attention was trained on what was generally labelled 'spin'. Now let's be accurate and let's bring in some of that logic I promised to employ. 'Spin' is, purely and simply, Propaganda. Addressed with the softer sounding term so as not to come across as sinister, because Propaganda is not a word you will ever hear used to describe content of Western operations, actions, strategies or words, unless you read Chomsky or similar authors. You will hear it when countries like Iran, or Russia, or Syria are being spoken about, and you will not hear it if countries such as Britain, or America, or even France or Germany, and so forth, are being spoken about.

That in itself - that right there, the use of one word for 'us' and another word for 'them' to create a subtle distinction between 'us' and 'them', is an actual example of Propaganda technique. Barely noticeable to an untrained or inexperienced eye.

So the likes of Tony's two heads of Propaganda, Peter Mandelson and Alastair Campbell, became labelled as 'spin doctors' instead. The softness of the word 'spin' connected with 'doctor', a word one associates with something more even than respectability - doctors are experts are they not? Spin Doctor! A title worthy of a black (naturally) business card, with swirly writing in gold leaf written on it with a quill.

It's Propaganda. The same thing.

Manipulation, control, filtered and censored and either brutally or subtly edited narratives (storylines) to give you precisely the information - the 'input' - that will give the desired 'outcome'. Garbage in, garbage out, as a computer programmer might say.

So behind his Cheshire Cat fascia, Tony Blair became as ruthless as you could fathom. While hiding behind his two assistants in Propaganda, who by all accounts acted as lightning rods to neutralise negativity and preserve his carefully designed and manufactured image. The success of this earned him the nickname of 'Teflon Tony'. Whatever he did, he got away with, nobody could make anything stick. In George Galloway's excellent film 'The Killing$ Of Tony Blair', it is alleged that he became corrupt, trading policy for cash. It was also claimed that he spoke the words "smile at everybody, and get someone else to stab them in the back", and then also that he worked closely with the likes of Rupert Murdoch in controlling media content. Propaganda in full, devious flow.

In addition, Tony Blair claims to be religious. I am not sure how one aligns that with illegal war and mass murder, but I am an atheist and therefore would not have the necessary knowledge to explain such a thing. His partner in international crime, George W. Bush, 43rd President of the United States no less, claims to be religious too. As someone who applies sound logical principles to everything, to me all of that is all a blur of baffled contradiction, untruths, hypocrisy and again, trying to manufacture a respectable front that isn't actually there. But a few things are beyond doubt;

there are massive amounts of wealth to accumulate, especially if you can act without morality or guilt. The machinations and manipulations of the geopolitical stage are dark and murky. War for profit and the so-called 'military industrial complex' are a reality and always have been. The dice are always loaded. And we see that these and other well-known devout Christians have demonstrated that unflappable faith is not necessarily an obstacle to operating highly profitably in that amoral psychosphere.

Tony Blair's most enduring legacy is, of course, the Iraq War. The notorious Weapons of Mass Destruction smoke-screen dossier used to justify an invasion that Blair and Bush had allegedly planned for more than a year, where no such weapons were found, as if anybody actually expected any to be found. As always with Western acts of aggression, we were told that there was simply not enough time to go through the United Nations, the body that any other country would be expected to consult with, and perhaps find obstacles in doing so. The West does not use channels where an obstacle might appear, nor delay. Nor will we hear it called aggression, another word only used in the context of vilification of other regimes. And Western leaders are conveniently unaccountable for anything that they perpetrate, they use the United Nations for the purpose of holding other countries and leaders to account, unless those regimes are big enough and have the appropriate weaponry to be as unaccountable themselves.

The way that George W. Bush and Tony Blair played the world like a proverbial violin, brings to mind the words of Herman Goering at the Nuremberg Trials. The

Nazis used Propaganda extremely effectively in an uncannily, though obviously coincidentally and unintentionally, identical fashion. The difference being, of course, that our violence was simply necessary for the security of the world. You know, in the same way that the bombings, and the instantaneous melting or vaporising - according to their distance from the blasts - of the innocent civilians of Nagasaki and Hiroshima, in the August of 1945, and the estimated 200,000 deaths, were also unavoidably necessary for the security of the world. War can be ugly, we are told. However, there is quite some difference between the deaths of women and children as what is known as collateral damage, abhorrent and unacceptable in itself, and making innocent civilians the actual target of a premeditated, genocidal, mass-murderous act. One bomb would, of course, have served the required purpose, and so the pointless waste of lives was unnecessarily amplified. You see, there were two different types of device to observe the effectiveness of, and so what better way to confirm that they both worked.

Goering's actual words were these:

"Naturally, the common people don't want war, neither in Russia nor in England nor in America, nor for that matter in Germany. That is understood. But the people can always be brought to the bidding of the leaders. That is easy. All you have to do is tell them they are being attacked, and denounce the pacifists for lack of patriotism and exposing the country to danger. It works the same way in every country."

It makes you wonder whether certain people had read these very words, with the aim of learning a useful skill from an expert teacher. I will conclude the passage about Teflon Tony with a schoolroom question:

Hands up boys and girls, who thinks it is appropriate that the only country that has ever actually used nuclear weapons to wipe out entire cities full of innocent people, in history, should be the one that decides which other countries should have access to such destructive power? (Countries which could then also unilaterally decide to commit similar atrocities, when they decide it is unavoidably necessary, to protect their interests, in exactly the same way as Harry S. Truman did in 1945).

The distractions are everywhere. Look through them, beyond them. The objective of mainstream media is to sell stories and not to inform.

Cameron, David. (Prime Minister 2010 - 2016)

If the legacy of Tony Blair was the media manipulation and the Iraq War, David Cameron's was the 'austerity' regime; and the austerity regime, in terms of its economic functionality, or more accurately its lack of functionality, has never been properly examined in the mainstream media at all. Gideon 'George' Osborne, (Magdalen College, Oxford, modern history) is not, never was, and never will be an economist nor a financial expert, but he was, is, or whatever, David Cameron's Bullingdon Club chumster, and so remained in the post of Chancellor Of The Exchequer for 6 years without - in my and many others' opinions - showing at any point, or over any period, capability at the job. It's who you know, you know. Plus, the currency of longevity in politics is obedience. Yet again the media abdicating responsibility and like Mr. Osborne, not doing their job. I'm going to dissect it - and I am not an economist either, but one can locate and investigate pretty much anything if one wants, especially with regard to something that is not, in demands on one's capacity for logic, even all that difficult to understand.

Austerity has always been explained, portrayed, framed, on the television, in the Press, in any broad public outlet, in completely inaccurate and incorrect ways, suggesting treating the country's economy as if it behaves in ways that it does not actually behave in. David Cameron had at least the 'E' element of his PPE to call upon, even if his history-graduate, party-club friend had no economic education or experience, and of course there are numerous economists to consult if need be. Maybe economists were consulted, but I would be surprised if any self-respecting, highly qualified, economist worth their salt would put their name to the austerity agenda. Unless they didn't care about ruining their reputation. A few have made unconvincing murmurs, but they are few and far between.

Before going further, here is the name of an eminent economist whose voice, and unrivalled expertise, is a most excellent starting point for delving into the subject matter:

Ann Pettifor. Cue search engine utilisation.

Ann is an expert in both economic and financial systems whose credentials would take me the best

part of an hour just to type out. Why a Chancellor Of The Exchequer, with no specific knowledge of the landscape, would not call Ann on the first day of the job, only George Osborne knows. But I have never seen him asked any kind of question from that angle. Surprise, surprise. Media omission alarm.

To relay Ann Pettifor's extensive economic understanding is a huge job, so I will humbly distil it down to very basic models which are not complicated. The likes of George Osborne and David Cameron, in the genius strategy of austerity, would have us believe that the economy operates like a household budget. A household has its income, and in order to operate without incurring debt, the expenditure is made to fit within what comes in. On a household level, it works perfectly well.

However. The economy of the so-called United Kingdom, or any country's economy, does not work in that way. And so, by giving us an over-simplistic and incorrect analogy, we are told that all the taxation, of different types, is the economy's income, and that we therefore have to budget within that in order to have a successful economy. The truth is completely different, actually the polar opposite. Taxation is not the economy's income at all. Taxation revenue is the **resulting** income from the economy, which has to be fuelled by investment, in all the correct areas where it will then generate the taxation revenues. Namely infrastructure projects and development, creating jobs and therefore income tax. The workers also spend money and so increase the amount of VAT income to the Treasury. They buy houses and pay stamp duty.

The businesses and shops where they spend the money then have more revenue too, and they pay their taxes on that. And then, the economy is able to actually grow and flourish. The infrastructure is strong and the taxation revenue grows. Austerity, on the other hand, tackles things the wrong way round which causes the economy to shrink. It administers cuts, so jobs are lost, and taxation revenue drops. And not surprisingly, the infrastructure therefore also weakens at the same time. For example, how can cuts to police budgets, and in turn therefore manpower numbers, result in anything other than a reduction in the safety of the population? Isn't it strange how terrorist incidents have materialised and increased in the last few years? One can always try blaming the London Mayor, as many xenophobes - racists - do, which is the equivalent of blaming a teacher for a cut in the budget of a school. But of course he is also a Muslim, which, in the eyes of the many idiots and racists and the Propaganda they consume, means he must be unworthy of trust.

Another example of the manipulation and distortion of the economic narrative is the matter of borrowing. The Conservatives have thrown around rhetoric about borrowing as if it were a terrible thing, irresponsible, one of the main stones that they throw at the Labour Party's approach is that it is not sound economics, and so Labour cannot be trusted on the economy. That is ridiculous and it is also incorrect, especially considering the myopic stupidity of the economic policy the Tories have been implementing. So.

171

Borrowing, at the household level, is generally not a healthy thing to do, debt for debt's sake is not a sound

strategy. The main reason being that individuals are charged high rates of interest on loans. But at the national level, borrowing is only bad if the wrong things are done with the money. If the right things are done with it, which in general they have not been, it can be very positive. George Osborne either didn't know, or didn't say. It could frankly be either or both, I wouldn't bet either way on that one. Governments are the lowest risk possible for banks to lend to - with some exceptions, yes - but the British government are not considered a risk , and so they are able to borrow money at very low rates compared to the family model. Money obtained through this channel can be invested into infrastructure, consider the example of building a hospital; vast numbers of builders, electricians, plumbers, painter/decorators, heating engineers, glaziers, flooring workers, to name just a few, are employed to build it. All of them pay their income tax and VAT, and give money to retail businesses, tradesmen and so on, who also pay their own tax on their revenue. At the end of the project, a new hospital exists. This adds huge value to the area in non-financial terms, treating and saving the lives of people of course, plus there are now a large number of doctors, nurses, porters, cleaners, caterers, et cetera, all of whom pay income tax, VAT, and give revenue to others, there is a pattern here is there not? Borrowing money to invest in projects like this, or schools, where similar logic applies, build infrastructure, the morale of and service to the public in general, and generate substantial taxation revenues right through the entire economy. And that added value is permanent. If money is borrowed but then 'invested' through financial systems instead,

which is mostly, and highly irresponsibly, what is done at present, with its risks and with no tangible benefits to the people, then of course none of those positive effects occur. Austerity squeezes the entire machine instead, and is financially, and economically, destructive and degenerative. The stated 'responsible economic management' is a false and dysfunctional model, that in point of fact brings about an unhealthy, progressively shrinking economy.

Let me pitch a scenario at this point. If a Cabinet were to contain, for example, an exceptional economist such as Ann Pettifor instead of a university drinking and vomiting buddy as Chancellor, a Home Secretary who has been, say, a Chief Constable rather than a geography graduate, a Foreign Secretary with years of experience as a diplomat at the highest level, such as an Ambassador, a Health Secretary who is a distinguished - retired probably, to accept the job - surgeon, or top NHS director, a Transport Secretary that has worked on the building projects of motorways or railways for years, an Education Secretary who has been a brilliant head teacher of a high-performing school, and so on - just imagine the quality of the decisions, ideas, achievements and outcomes that might result. But instead we get given a room full of history (or similarly unrelated subject) graduates that have become career politicians. It would be a great joke if it were funny, but it's not in the least funny because it's actually what really happens. High-ranking experts, at the top of all the various speciality departments, that report to bosses that are just politicians, no expertise. But if all you are doing is subtracting from budgets, then obviously you don't need any knowledge, just the use of a calculator - and you'd be so important, powerful and famous that you could delegate all that. I wish it were me telling the lies this time.

In summary. Cabinet posts are not given to people on merit, or relevant experience, qualifications or background, they are given to career politicians by Prime Ministers who have reached the position themselves by virtue of the same principles, who are perhaps friends, regardless of specialist knowledge, experience or career path, and most importantly, in general, that will toe the line and be loyal to policy. In other words, do as they're told. Those are the attributes that put somebody into such a position. Politics. By definition. A self-perpetuating machine of people whose experience is irrelevant to the jobs they are asked to do, so we shouldn't be surprised when things are done badly. It continues to a crass, farcical level when 'Cabinet reshuffles' occur, the very name describes what happens; people generally unsuited to one job, and so delivering generally mediocre results, are moved to a different department, which is also not something they have advanced knowledge of either. Education Secretary becomes Health Secretary. Home Secretary moves to Foreign Secretary. Musical chairs. The little club rearranges to a different permutation, they sit in a different chair at Cabinet meetings so that they can look out of different windows during the more boring bits. The same faces are shown to the electorate so that they are perceived to be **good at everything!**

A complete circus. We British people are so used to it that the abject madness of it gets missed, and we don't have mainstream commentators pointing any of it out- as usual. In the end you have to write a book yourself. Which takes ages.

……..

Now here is something that is really worth pointing out. If you are a career politician without a clue about the intricacies, or the operational and human challenges within your designated department, be it health, education, environment, transport and so on - there is a profoundly important fact that even the history graduates can understand, and by necessity, hide behind.

Those that report to you DO know what they're doing.

--.

(So the untalented get a piggy-back ride on the more able).

……..

And make no mistake about who will jump to take the credit, and bask in the bright sunlight of career advancement and Right-Wing tabloid sycophancy.

It's a house of cards, that no-one gives a nudge to.

Nobody.

Because everybody wants to keep it.

It is obviously no wonder that scientists, mathematicians, doctors, project managers, head teachers, real specialists of many kinds are not asked to do such jobs. They'd be too efficient and would disagree with things that don't make any sense, and would look at the problems and solve them rather than just be told what to do and say in public. The more profound point though, is would they accept the jobs anyway? Since the actual skills are not expected to be involved, just PR, and rehearsed speeches, and all the rest of the silly out-of-place dynamics. Those experts, meanwhile, are studying to explain the universe, or solving medical issues and finding cures to save lives, or taking care of pupils so that they then achieve and over-achieve their potential. People, of ability and integrity, and so they do not have the correct skill set or attitude for the waffle, bluster, rhetoric and superficial and immature theatre of politics.

Perhaps David Cameron understood all of this or perhaps he didn't, PPE or not. But he didn't do anything about it, like every other Prime Minister of the so-called United Kingdom also hasn't.

....

David Cameron will also be remembered as the Prime Minister that facilitated the referendum about whether to leave the EU, which without any shadow of a doubt was a monstrous mistake. The complications, of many kinds, that the resulting can of worms gave rise to, will have repercussions far into the future and without it, perhaps we would still be able to use the term 'United Kingdom' with a straight face, whereas now it is an inaccurate and meaningless term.

And so, in the beautiful ancient halls and quadrangles of the universities of Oxford and Cambridge, right now, the skewed machine's cells are duplicating and multiplying, and the system is not changing one bit. Politicians and intellectuals, and ne'er the twain shall meet.

May, Theresa. (Prime Minister 2016 -)

To place Theresa May, with her undergraduate knowledge of geography, in a section entitled 'Strategic Styles', is not really accurate in the same way that it is with the other individuals within this topic. Her 'style' does not exist in the way Tony Blair's does, or David Cameron's or Margaret Thatcher's, there is not the coherence of approach. Admittedly she has not had the length of time in power than those others did, but I doubt that would make the slightest difference.

The only thread of continuity that there is to categorise her, is that she is unbelievably self-serving, of which there is no shortage of evidence and example. I will therefore refer to the pertinent facts and then the conclusion is there to draw. It should also be noted that she has been very much defined as the Brexit Prime Minister, and the necessity of addressing that gargantuan, and some would say impossible, for anybody, issue has overshadowed everything she has done. But then, she did decide that she wanted to tackle it, poisoned chalice though everyone but she could clearly see it was. The sultry magnet of power distorted her eyesight. Sound judgement has never been necessary for, nor often found in, British Prime Ministers. After speeches she made in support of remaining in the European Union, her chasing, and getting, the job of delivering the opposite, was not overly surprising to see.

Our portrait of Theresa May was formed by the six years she spent as Home Secretary in David Cameron's Cabinet. We saw her patronise, and disrespect, and show contempt for the entire police force, which was her main area of responsibility, delivering to them some of the most cringeworthy speeches one might ever see or hear. She disrespected them and they naturally returned the compliment. She was sheepishly obeying the instructions of the Bullingdon Twins and imposing cuts, and reforms that were basically simply more cuts, over the entire period. As I insinuated earlier, if politicians do as they are told they keep their jobs longer, Theresa May and George Osborne were in the same positions for the whole of David Cameron's time in office. Obedience pays off in politics as I asserted earlier.

She was quite happy, in return for the appointment as Leader of the Conservative Party and, therefore, Prime Minister, to ditch her support of remaining in the European Union to negotiate for leaving instead. Fickle and brazenly hypocritical values indeed. Power does things to people, mostly not positive things.

She was, through Philip Hammond's budget of Spring 2017, to bring in a policy that meant that the self-employed would pay higher National Insurance contributions, in direct opposition to the wording of the 2015 Conservative Manifesto, not that that is inconsistent with the behaviour of a politician - however the public backlash caused her to cancel the move, a U-turn and a glaring show of weakness and self-conscious appeasement. Not exactly strong or stable leadership.

She had said in recent times that she favoured Britain leaving the European Convention of Human Rights. She claimed it "made us less secure". When she stood for the leadership of her party she dropped the idea, and said so within the Conservative Manifesto at the General Election in 2017. Once again, no gumption to carry ideas through, which is not something one could usually level at other Prime Ministers. She seems to scare very easily and run. She very successfully displayed a spine as brittle as a dried-up twig.

And speaking of the General Election of 2017……..

After announcing that there would be no snap election, in March of 2017, a snap election was called on the 18th April. It was to take place on the 8th June. ("In April May calls June election" was virally touted around the social media platforms). That U-turn was either a lie, or another example of a whimsical, flippant, indecisive and unfocused mind. The only reason that could be seen as feasible for calling the election, as the Conservatives were somehow, astonishingly, still quite popular, was that she felt she could improve on that popularity and have a stronger mandate in Brexit negotiations. Not that it would have affected or altered the fact that the European Union possessed all the leverage to negotiate with, even though the blatant lies of the Leave campaign made voters believe the opposite. Bulldogs' tails had never wagged quite so excitedly.

The seven weeks that followed defined her, and in ways that she did not foresee nor want.

Theresa May's election campaign, if one could use the term, was quite a spectacle.

She refused to participate in any live TV leaders' debates, stating the reason as wanting to "spend her time out speaking to the public". It is doubtful that the excuse for an excuse convinced a single person in the country. Her fear and cowardice was palpable. She was labelled as spineless once again by the majority of commentators.

While she was out speaking to the public, she would only address voters that were already going to vote for her anyway, and supporters of other parties, and journalists, were not permitted to attend. Very risk-averse, is as polite as one can be about that approach. Spineless, again, was levelled. That same brittle twig.

The speeches that she gave to those hand-picked audiences, were virtually identical, and therefore completely rehearsed and memorised. One thing that a leader of a country should essentially have in their arsenal, I would have thought, is the ability to speak without learning scripts, at least sometimes. We saw that it was pointless for interviewers to use secondary probes (follow-up or clarification questions) because she does not give interviewers the respect of answering them, she prefers, or is only able, to repeat her memorised words. A well-trained parrot could do the job just as well. That wooden delivery is still with her to this day, as is her constant insistence of starting most of her sentences with the word - the letter - "I".

She, or one of her most creative and supremely clever advisers, probably with a degree in PPE, coined a little slogan that she would repeat *ad infinitum* and *ad nauseam,* which was 'strong and stable'. She used it to refer to the government, but specifically her government, and so she was describing herself with it also - therefore she made it into a presidential-style campaign of personalities. It turned the spotlight directly onto herself, making demands of her that she was not remotely up to delivering. 'Strong and stable' quickly became a big joke, and sadly she continued to use the phrase long after everybody was laughing at it.

The memorised speech was also full of barbed insults of her opponent, Jeremy Corbyn, and the irony was embarrassingly evident. The way one cringes when watching Basil Fawlty put his foot in things and dig holes for himself to fall into. Her framing of the election campaign as being about personalities, backfired, because Jeremy Corbyn is a man of honesty and integrity, and grew in stature and popularity throughout the campaign in the exact way that she thought that she would. Often a question about a completely unrelated topic would be answered with insulting references about Mr. Corbyn. It was entertaining, but in a very cruel and voyeuristic manner that actually made one feel guilt, sadness and compassion.

She had the brass neck to level that Jeremy Corbyn's socialist agenda was financially irresponsible and undeliverable, which with correct economic management is totally untrue, as I explained before. She claimed "there is no Magic Money Tree", unwittingly laying the foundations for her biggest hypocritical fall of them all.

Conversely, footage of Jeremy Corbyn's campaign in motion, showed a completely different approach. He engaged genuinely with people. No rigid, word-for-word rehearsed speeches. No rules as to who he would talk to and not talk to. Happy to take, and actually answer, any questions on any subject. Informally walking around neighbourhoods chatting to the residents, and listening to them as well. Listening more than talking when appropriate; 'we have two ears and one mouth', as the well-known saying goes.

All the time that Jeremy Corbyn was conducting an inclusive campaign while Theresa May conducted her exclusive one, his popularity soared, while she carried on embarrassingly like the aforementioned parrot. Insulting a hugely popular man, who even in the face of her nasty comments, in voice and in print, never once made any of it personal. His principles forbade him to, and as I said he is a man with a level of integrity not usually found in a politician, and so he did not stoop to the same depths of the filthy and putrid gutter that Theresa May, and much of the typically and predictably slanted and abusive media, had been inhabiting.

The result on the 8th June 2017 was not a surprise to any Labour Party voter, nor was it a surprise to anybody that followed the madness of the two diametrically executed campaigns with objectivity.
She had single-handedly, in making the whole campaign about herself and not assembling and deploying a team, eroded virtually the whole advantage that was in place before the election was even called. Her party were largely furious about it though most of them stayed quietly fuming. She now had much less of a mandate, not more.

What she did next was absolutely incredible, when I speak of self-serving this is the most extreme example of what I mean. The government had needed 326 seats for a majority in the House Of Commons, but only achieved 318. She was on thin ice, but such was her determination to stay in her job, she decided to recruit the 10 seats won by the Democratic Unionist Party of Northern Ireland. That would make 328 seats for crucial votes, and a slim majority to pass legislation with, and she would stay Prime Minister on just fractionally thicker ice.

As I explained earlier, she frantically checked her bank balance at the cashpoint, and was dismayed to discover that she was a few pence short of the £1 billion, or the £1.5 billion, or whatever the exact amount was, to make the decisive bribe. So instead, she improvised and bribed the DUP with British taxpayers' money. That is what you call determination to get a result at any cost. How on Earth is such a thing allowed in a so-called developed country? And look at what else she was making clear - there had been a Magic Money Tree there all the time, she had just lied about it.

One that is not there to help or house homeless people, but is there to buy a few votes in Parliament.

One that is not there to treat the epidemic of mental health sufferers, but is there to buy nuclear missiles.

One that is not there for scientific research, but is there to give blank cheques to MPs or royals for their seemingly unlimited expenses and costs.

The scale of the outrage if Jeremy Corbyn had done something so disgusting would have been monumental, except the very point is that he would never do such a despicable and dishonest thing. But often British voters prefer to elect the shadiest characters. Theresa May, in absolute, proud, self-contradictory mode, was the one levelling the factually false accusations that Mr. Corbyn could not be trusted to take care of the public purse. You couldn't make it up.

What is that awful, overpowering stench?

It is the unmistakable pong of the bullshit of hypocrisy. The Magic Money Tree has its roots growing all the way through it. In fact, hypocrisy and money can often be very tricky to separate and untangle.

The risk and irresponsibility of Theresa May's selfish stunt ran to much more than just the money and the seats, too. Northern Ireland's history is full of troubles, violence, territorial and religious hatred, up until relatively recently. Murders, bombings and punishment beatings were commonplace, perpetrated and suffered by both sides of the conflict. After long and very difficult discussions and negotiations, peace was agreed, and the terms were enshrined in a sacred treaty that brought about and maintained the peace between Northern Ireland and the Republic of Ireland in the South. It became known as the Good Friday Agreement, signed on the 10th April 1998 and effective from 2nd December 1999. A great many people had worked for a very long time to put it together, decades in fact, and it not only massively improved life for many Irish folk, but has without any doubt at all saved a significant number of actual Irish and British lives, literally. No longer is "running through a wheatfield" the 'naughtiest thing' Theresa May ever did. She could easily have put lives at risk, which is even more unforgivable and stupid than the bribe. All for her own personal gains. As I said, Prime Ministers can still land the job without sound judgement, there's some cast-iron proof of it.

Amber Rudd proved expendable, collateral damage, and very much a sacrificial lamb, a ritual blood offering, one presumes, to the Dark Lord Satan, if Mrs. May's soulless actions in general are anything to go by. After a number of embarrassments that were caused by public revelations of lies, Amber Rudd resigned from her post as Home Secretary in April 2018, ultimately over the mismanagement of the 'Windrush scandal', where crucial documents and data were found to be missing, flagged by incorrect deportation instructions to children of Commonwealth citizens. However, Amber Rudd had only been in the post for less than two years - the previous Home Secretary, for over six years, had been the one and only Theresa May, who stayed very quiet regarding any culpability for the crisis, not that (as usual) I saw any such questions asked of her personally - and so true to form, the media did absolutely nothing to hold her to account and research the history of the matter. Perhaps we have a 'Teflon Theresa' situation, or a biased media, I know where my bets are placed. Most likely of all, secret arrangements were made so that Rudd fell on her sword under the promise of a return to the Cabinet, which, lo and behold, took place in November 2018. Does anyone with an iota of intelligence really get persuaded or convinced by any political narrative at face value? I am sure they don't, but then I did use the qualifying phrase "with an iota of intelligence" - and therein lies the rub, the absolute, depressing crux of the matter. We have so many gullible idiots in this so-called United Kingdom that believe what they see and hear without questioning a thing.

Mrs. May's flagrant, self-serving actions do seem to have no boundaries. Though integrity is not a word that appears in the Official Conservative Party English Dictionary, or OCPED. They'd never have cause to use it if it was. The word coward however, certainly does appear in the OCPED, for use in describing an individual that has a twig-spine, will not participate in a live TV debate, or even an open meeting in a General Election campaign, preferring to stay all safely wrapped up in cotton wool somewhere cosy, yet still not be able to win people over and achieve a result.

When I said a little earlier that "you couldn't make it up", that wasn't really true, you could. I also, of course, made up the notion of an Official Conservative Party English Dictionary. An ocped is actually a rare species of octopus that lives on land, scuttling restlessly on the tips of its eight tentacle-feet in its habitat on a remote, and barely inhabited, Pacific island. It is so scarce, secretive and shy that it has never been photographed, which is why it is not well known.

<u>Thatcher, Margaret. (Prime Minister 1979 - 1990)</u>

Discussions and opinions about Margaret 'Baroness' Thatcher appear to become shrouded in a mythological and mystical mist of legend. But then, that is often the case with dragons.

My opinion of her is that she was the worst and most irresponsible Prime Minister ever to take office. And every opinion I hold on every person or subject that I have an opinion about, I can back up with a whole raft of hard facts and irrefutable logic and evidence, which I will proceed to do without delay.

The first fact to remind ourselves of is that Margaret Thatcher was rejected after her application to Oxford. That is not the case with any other Oxford Alumnus that I have mentioned. Her place was offered when somebody else pulled out. Let's not start from a position of thinking she was some breed of mythological or mystical dragon genius, or modern day prophetess, because she was absolutely nothing of the sort - even though an elementary command of a science subject would logically put one's brainpower ahead of an advanced command of history or PPE, and Margaret Thatcher, while still Margaret Roberts, did study chemistry. And in my opinion she would have had tougher opposition for a place due to her subject choice, as I touched on previously. I mean, that was my subject. I jest. And as a science student, guess what? She had been to a state school. It all fits doesn't it.

Margaret Thatcher's strategy, which went under the smoke-screen, or camouflage, definition of 'monetarism', was nothing more than a car boot sale of every government asset she could lay her grubby mitts on, and I will break that down into bite-sized chunks shortly. Her personal style, to be extremely generous in calling it that, was that of a 500-ton steamroller squashing anything that tried to stop it in its trajectory, which some would call leadership, and I would concede that within very specific boundaries and parameters one could, at a stretch, call it such. That is the only thing approaching a compliment - and if you read it carefully it was no such thing anyway - that I am able to say about Mrs. Thatcher. The rest formulates my assertions about her legacy, and I hope it is as damning as I intend it to be. Speaking of damnation, if there were an actual place of eternal torture and agony, few people, if any, in history would be ahead of her in qualification for it. The fellow war criminal club members could crawl, beg and plead for mercy alongside her for first place in the infernal queue. If 'war criminal' even applies to her, which is very much an unresolved point even today. But some would concur.

Before going any further, I will make a highly relevant point for the attention of those who might say that it is not fair to criticise somebody who is not in a position to respond, Mrs. Thatcher having been dead for a few years now. Secrecy legislation, really in existence to protect information that protects the country, has been abused for as long as it has existed, and Mrs. Thatcher used secrecy legislation to hide documents and evidence, for 30 year periods - yes she used it more than once - purely to protect herself, her image and her underhand actions and lies. I will describe how shortly. Anyway, therefore, when she deliberately used such powers in cynical ways, for entirely selfish and devious covering up of evidence, then she herself has invited judgement after her death, the information was deliberately intended to come out after she had died. So I need not justify matters any further.

There is a term often used, 'the family silver', to refer to assets passed down as heirlooms within families, from generation to generation. In the literal case of valuable artefacts and objects, they have either sentimental value, financial value, or often both, but if sold the vendor only receives a capital value, a single price. They do not in general have a yield of income as well as the value of the item or items. Even then, when the term 'selling the family silver' is used, it is usually a critical term implying that somebody has sold off something precious. Priceless is the context, generally. Irresponsible, parting with something irreplaceable, as it has then gone and the asset is no longer within the family.

189

Margaret Thatcher disposed of the country's family silver in the most spectacularly irresponsible fashion. Over 50 state-owned businesses were sold off, and these particular assets had both capital value and also yielded income, the businesses brought huge revenue into the coffers of the Treasury. She certainly did not do anything clever whatsoever in enacting this crude and cynically opportunistic strategy, it was the polar opposite of that. She claimed that privatisation was desirable because it was "one of the central means of reversing the corrosive and corrupting effects of socialism", which was absolutely false, in fact socialism is just about taking care of people, a different and more human approach than letting the entire economy run on market forces, capitalism. In fact both communism, which is an extreme version of socialism, but not the same thing as greatly biased commentators would have us believe, and capitalism are both corrosive and corrupting systems, which end up with an undesirable situation of elites with all the money and power, and a population that are trodden down. Mrs. Thatcher's rhetoric was based on incorrect assumptions, and in describing privatisation in such a way, she duped the British people by making it an ideology. The toxic outcomes for the future of Britain were colossal.

Mrs. Thatcher's ideology can be illustrated by a quote of hers:

"I do not know anyone who has gotten to the top (whatever 'the top' is) without hard work. That is the recipe. It will not always get you to the top, but it will get you pretty near."

This ethos is highly flawed but still prevalent in Britain now. To strip it to the bare bones, if you are successful, wealthy, you deserve it, and if you are poor, you deserve that. It is ridiculously over-simplistic, because there are a great many relevant variables and factors that can apply, and whilst there is some truth in her comment, it is full of holes. The thing about senior politicians is that they know that their comments will be given out publicly, and any lie, half-truth, can be thrown at the people and if it is persuasive, people will believe it. Not all people, not those with a few brain cells and some insight for example - but often enough people to give the politician a decent swathe of public opinion. All politicians exploit that dynamic ruthlessly. The stronger the words, "corrosive and corrupting" in this example, the more impact it can create. It doesn't have to be remotely true or accurate, only the effect and the impact matter, as with the vacuous, dishonest, misleading Brexit Leave campaign you could say.

Here are just a few of the state-owned businesses that she that off, sacrificing all of the revenues that they generated for the government. No more than a jumble sale of the country's family silver, afterwards permanently and irretrievably gone;

British Aerospace (1981 - 51.57% sold).

Cable & Wireless (1981, 1983 and 1985).

British Telecom (1984).

British Gas (1986).

191

British Steel (1987).

British Airways (1987).

Rolls-Royce (1987).

Rover Group, previously British Leyland (1988).

There is no point in giving a more exhaustive list, the intentions are as clear as day. She did not care that she was selling the family silver because she was only going to be in power for a few years, and so the capital values came in during her time in office, and the future beyond that was going to be somebody else's problem. The same process of thought as hiding documents for 30 years that would have shown her true colours, however she only just cheated their publication while she was alive, by dying only a few months before they became public in 2014.

—·—

A public official, that should therefore be accountable for all of their actions, cheating, through the abuse of legislation that exists for a wholly different purpose, in order to avoid accountability. In exactly the same fashion as the example I referred to in the previous of these passages, about Princess Margaret and the film that was made about her misdemeanours. Nobody finds out until after the perpetrator is dead and so escapes all consequences. Utterly dishonest and outrageous behaviour that should have protective protocols to follow to prevent such abuses of the powers, but elites have such facilities in place to ensure the absence of accountability, and there is zero chance of it being changed.

One such time specifically refers to documents related to her handling of the miners' strike, and shows the extent of her collusion to discredit the character of the National Union of Mineworkers' leader Arthur Scargill, also the cover-up of plans to close collieries, which made clear that Arthur Scargill's accusations, which she vigorously denied, were actually true and it was her that was lying. There were other documents, made secret under the same 30-year rule, from 1979 when she first took office, that she hid for her own personal benefit. Abuses of power everywhere you look. The theatre production 'Coal' by Gary Clarke gives a wonderful caricature of Mrs. Thatcher as a grotesque, tyrannical, scowling witch that treads on people, specifically the coal industry and communities of Yorkshire, a place very dear to my heart, where folks have a personal sense of honour that Margaret Thatcher could not possibly comprehend. It is a place where society is a real thing, contrary to her ridiculous stated opinion, that eliminates all possibility that she had a heart beating in her chest. The people of Yorkshire know and remember exactly what she was like, and capable of. There is no love lost there over Margaret Thatcher and justifiably so.

So to the actual method of selling the family silver. The processes of the flotations of many of these companies were about as cynical as you could possibly invent, and they were basically as follows; the public were allowed to participate in buying shares of the privatised companies. But the share prices offered were based on undercuts of the actual valuations of the shares. Therefore, on the day of the sale, members of the public obtained an asset that was immediately worth a higher value than they had paid. And so, a great many people, to whom share ownership was a novel, new concept, made a 'quick buck' by selling them straight away. Made possible due to the deliberate discount. For lots of people, it was a freebie, a few quid in the back pocket, and therefore hugely popular in spite of the underhand philosophy underpinning the entire strategy. It won votes, and the cheap bribe that it actually was seemed largely irrelevant. A veritable bargain basement. What's more, this method was employed with a number of the privatisations. And who did these multitudes sell their shares to? Private investors, hovering around like vultures, knowing that there was still a great investment in those assets. That outcome was not obvious to most people, as the whole idea was new to them - but the vultures were well aware, and so, of course, was the Right Honourable Margaret Hilda Thatcher. I have not looked into whether any of those vultures were, perhaps, Conservative Party donors, or perhaps personal friends or acquaintances of Mrs. Thatcher's, I would doubt it, because it smells of corruption, and we don't have any corruption in the corridors of power of the so-called United Kingdom. The morning papers would, of course, immediately tell us if there was anything wrong.

Or am I just being stupidly naive, or maybe a conspiracy theorist madman? Possibly both, but there was a definite impression of wholesale and sinister subterfuge and some people getting very rich behind the scenes.

I detect, again, the overpowering stench of bullshit on the air, mixed - as is often the case - with the

194

irresistible and seductive aroma of money. I didn't notice any critical media hammering of Mrs. Thatcher, or the entire strategy, either. There is definitely a theme of media silence on certain matters that recurs and recurs.

It is my firm belief that if she felt she could have got away with it, she would have privatised the entire NHS, but realised it was a step much, much too far at the time. Yet, in 2019, after many stealthily introduced changes within the operations of the NHS, a great many functions are now carried out and provided by private companies. More and more of them, in fact, as time progresses. It is called the internal market, which at least approaches honesty in definition. But that is not the most interesting thing about these developments. The most interesting part is that politicians, many of whom are involved in the decision-making process in their capacity as ministers, sit on the boards of the very same companies. Should that even be legal, tolerated, allowed in any way whatsoever? Maybe that one falls within a definition of corruption, or perhaps the diluted - but identical in inference - 'conflict of interest'. It seems to go on in most countries in the world, why not the so-called United Kingdom? We are told that such a market place encourages and delivers higher levels of efficiency - yet it is difficult to imagine how, since private companies are obligated to deliver both profits and dividends to shareholders somehow, while they fulfil their 'more efficient' contracts. It doesn't add up, does it? But then, the suggestions of the ethereal, invisible, nebulous 'higher efficiency' has come from the squeaky-clean voices of slimy politicians, so why would we expect it to be true. Newly appointed secretaries of state always tell us of inefficiency and the need to shake up the area they have been appointed to run, even though every previous incumbent has also said and acted identically.

There was another arm to the market-trader strategy of Mrs. Thatcher. She decided to sell off the rest of the family silver, the council houses. The spin, the Propaganda, was put out with the following context;

"we (with Mrs.Thatcher that's always actually 'I') believe that everybody should own their own home". It sounded so positive, so wonderful, people will lap it up she'll have been thinking, knowing that mass bribery had already been proven to work like a dream. The trickery motored on, unchecked, accompanied with language promising the angelic empowerment of ordinary people. It seemed like, as well as an automatic seat in the House Of Lords, a sainthood and a seat beside God were guaranteed, she was spreading so much celestial light and unselfish, altruistic goodwill. Excuse me while I briefly vomit into my coffee.

And so it came to pass that council house tenants were given the opportunity to purchase their rented properties, at discounted values, naturally. The longer the tenants had lived in their properties, the bigger the discount they were given. The Thatcher car boot sale rolled on unstoppably. All masked and wrapped up with her ideology of self-defined creation of wealth for ordinary people, when it was just the car boot sale I described. Once again, the assets left government permanently and brought in billions, but the discounts meant that the assets were almost given away, in as cynical an approach as had been applied in the privatisations of the state-owned companies. Once again as with the flotations, some tenants bought their houses cheaply and sold them immediately for profit, along with lots of free deadly asbestos in many cases. They will have made some money, and were happy enough with that, but once again, who bought them? There are numerous Conservative politicians that own large numbers of properties, and plenty of private companies with similar large portfolios run by, mostly, men within the same circles, networks, Masonic Lodges, golf club members, Bullingdon Club reunions, etc.

What is that smell? More horrible, stinking bullshit and more delightfully fragrant banknotes.

The Treasury, of course, was bulging with cash from the discounted disposal of all those assets, and only the short term was of interest to Mrs. Thatcher, as always, and to Hell with the future. In the same vein as the 30-year burial of embarrassing documents.

Here is another quote, where she shows her contempt for people having instincts towards the benefits of caring about others:

"There is no such thing as society: there are individual men and women, and there are families." Do I hear an echo of 'Divide And Conquer'?

There you have it, the official endorsement of 'I'm all right Jack', of 'me me me', and forget the welfare of other people, they don't matter.

Here is another:

"One of the things being in politics has taught me is that men are not a reasoned or reasonable sex."

She was probably trying to show a sense of humour that she didn't possess, to be fair, but gave an accidental glimpse of transparency into her dark soul.

And finally for this part of the topic, two final quotes:

"I don't mind how much my ministers talk - as long as they do what I say."

"I am extraordinarily patient provided I get my own way in the end."

Fans of Thatcher will claim those last two quotes as an illustration of her leadership qualities, after all - good leaders are sure of themselves - although the very best leaders are able to listen and evaluate as well as make decisions, or to be clearer, to make decisions after listening and not before. That is not something that she was able or willing to do, so she was in fact a poor leader in any subtle way.

A critic might go much further and suggest that those quotes are by nothing more than a dictator.

A psychiatrist might evaluate the quotes, and a great many other facets of her character, as those of a malignant narcissist, or perhaps of a psychopath, or at least a sociopath. She certainly merits a clinical description of one sort or another.

It is not possible, especially after saying that, to conclude a piece about Mrs. Thatcher without reference to the sinking of the cruiser the General Belgrano, during the Falklands conflict of 1982.

The Falkland Islands are a throwback to the British Empire, which like all empires, such as that of the Romans, Alexander The Great's or Genghis Khan's for example, refers to attempts to take over, and therefore to take possession of, as much land as possible. By force, inevitably.

The Falkland Islands are only 945 miles from Argentina, and some 7,896 miles from London, which shows clearly, using advanced arithmetic and geography, that the islands should be under the ownership of Britain and not Argentina. (I now need to state that that was sarcasm, in order that gloating smart-arses don't start suggesting that I had mistakenly put those the wrong way round. The sarcasm is aimed at those who did, and do, think that the islands should not be part of Argentina, by some strange and ridiculous logic). The islanders, anyway, consider themselves to be British, and so when the Argentinian General Leopoldo Galtieri ordered them to be occupied, while Mrs. Thatcher was in office, British armed forces were dispatched to reclaim them.

On 2nd May 1982, while situated outside the British-imposed exclusion zone around the islands (which had a radius of two hundred nautical miles), the cruiser the

199

General Belgrano was torpedoed and sunk. None of those facts are disputed. The disputed element is, whether though outside the zone it was a danger to our forces or not. There are compelling arguments both ways, so it remains disputed all the same. While 772 men were rescued from the water, 323 men were killed, 2 of whom were civilians.

Whether it was a war crime or not is also disputed, but then British leaders, like American leaders, do not get indicted or prosecuted for war crimes, that too is an undisputed fact which is still true in 2019.

On 24th May 1983, during the General Election campaign, Margaret Thatcher appeared on the BBC Nationwide programme, and famously took a question live on air from a Diana Gould regarding the sinking of the Belgrano. Mrs. Thatcher asserted, there and then, that the facts of the matter would be available in 30 years time. We are of course well aware of how fond she was of abusing that particular power.

Mrs. Gould was very persistent, and so was Mrs. Thatcher, and nothing was really resolved - although Mrs. Thatcher did appear to get very uncomfortable. However, despite her persistence, Mrs. Gould was not technically effective in her questioning, because Mrs. Thatcher was never pushed to justify her comments. She simply kept repeating that "it (the Belgrano) was a danger to our ships". The questions that unfortunately did not follow, were "in what way were they a danger?" and "what was your evidence to support your decision?" and "what other options were open to you?" Although, to be fair, such questions might well have just been answered, more accurately deflected or dodged, with further reference to, and therefore her hiding behind, the content that she had buried for 30 years. After all, the whole purpose behind the enactment of that privilege is to cover things up, whether it is right or wrong to do it. In Margaret Thatcher's case, the most generous one can be is to say that she used it for both right and for wrong. That 'cult status' interview clip can be found on the online site YouTube.

The act of the sinking of the Belgrano is sometimes called a war crime and equally disputed that it was not. It was a single incident, and so one has no facts to bear that would suggest that Margaret Thatcher was a wilful mass murderer. Personally, though I say once again I think she was the worst British Prime Minister in history on the evidence I have written about, I imagine it was a difficult decision that she probably took carefully and with correct motive. The kind of decision that military commanders would be able to, and no doubt do, take in such situations without the training of a public spotlight on their actions. Just because I think Margaret Thatcher was irresponsible, misguided, and without a shred of doubt totally dishonest when she wanted to be, does not mean I would extend the accusations to that of evil and malevolence. (My comments about her damnation were not serious, I don't believe in such codswallop). However - if one scrutinises the ruthlessness with which she approached the mining communities, or the motives behind all the privatisations, or the personal qualities displayed in the quotes, she was probably capable of almost anything, like a sociopath, or a psychopath, or a malignant narcissist, also is.

If it were a war crime, it pales into insignificance when viewed against the aforementioned actions of Tony Blair and George W. Bush, who in proof of my assertion will never be indicted or prosecuted for war crimes, even though many leaders that have committed far milder crimes will be and have been. The big machine has no tolerance for equality.

To add to the big Treasury pot, in addition to the selling off of companies, many of which were profitable, and the selling off of the council properties to tenants, and therefore the loss of all the rental incomes to councils, Mrs. Thatcher also was in office when the Snorre oil field was discovered in the North Sea in 1979, the Oseberg oil field and Troll gas field also in 1979, the Miller oil field in 1983, the Alba and Smorbukk in 1984, the Snohvit and Draugen also in 1984, and the Heidrun in 1985. Imagine how much more money rolled in.

Existentially, one observes that even sections of ocean and underground substances are deemed, somehow, to be able to belong to somebody, be they a government or an oil company. Companies at this very moment are trying to gain permission to indulge in 'fracking', whereby they drill into the earth, often in areas of natural beauty, having been given that permission by bodies that are supposed to be there to protect those areas. Of course austerity, which has a literal dictionary definition of 'harshness', has rendered many local government bodies almost penniless which hasn't helped the matter any. Generally, it is eventually members of the public that have to live in trees, or sit in front of machinery, to stop the two-fold abuse by the private company and the public local council.

So I would guess that Mrs. Thatcher's rampant but warped imagination and moneylust would soon have led to discounted offers to the British electorate to own square miles of ocean, or perhaps parts of the moon, or both. Perhaps cubic metres of air, and buckets of soil and desert sand. I suppose she just didn't have time to get around to selling it all.

So many monetisable commodities, so little time. She certainly tried very hard.

Thou Shalt Not Kill

Personally, like most people, I popped out of my mother's vagina knowing instinctively that I should not kill.

There was no need for the booming voice of a god.

There was no need to set a shrub on fire.

There was no need for a stone tablet with an inscription.

"Thou Shalt Not Kill", God said to Moses, and He then proceeded to set fire to a living bush.

....

I am not certain why the god in question didn't also feel any compulsion to advise men that "Thou Shalt Not Rape".

Or perhaps "Thou Shalt Treat Women As Equals".

It might have served great purpose, since in 2019 there is still not full equality, and there is certainly no shortage of rape.

A commandment might have helped to speed things up a little bit.

The only reference to a woman within the Ten Commandments is with the distinct context of her as the property of her husband ("thy neighbour's wife").

Universally, around the globe, all monotheistic religions agree that God is male.

It seems no coincidence that it is also universal that societies are male-dominated.

It is also indisputable, with any applications of logic, that the religious books were all written over many years by humans.

It is therefore not surprising that the males did not suggest that God could be a female Goddess, as it would compromise their dominance somewhat.

…·…

Why does anybody, let alone multitudes, attend a public execution?

Why does anybody, let alone multitudes, participate in a fox hunt?

Why does anybody, let alone multitudes, attend a bullfight?

…·…

Why does anybody hunt bears?

Why does anybody hunt lions?

Why does anybody hunt tigers?

Why does anybody hunt deer?

Why does anybody hunt any animal?

…·…

205

The precious 5th Amendment of the American Constitution was voted for in 1791.

How on Earth is it still hidden behind in 2019?

Which of today's high-powered weapons was available in 1791?

Why are people still taken seriously when they hide behind the words?

Why is that defence of guns, in 2019, granted even the slightest of credibility?

Why do I not see interviewers pointing out and pressuring on the question of how the 5th Amendment has no literal relevance in 2019?

When will it be updated, revised, rewritten in a modern context?

Shall we ask the NRA to explain how that can be called insignificant?

....

How many other innocents need to be slaughtered by angry young men in schoolrooms and colleges?

Why is it always young men and not young women that carry out such massacres?

Does anybody even care?

Are the underlying social causes and issues ever going to be isolated and addressed?

Will it make any difference at all if angry young women start to follow the boys' lead and jump on the murderous bandwagon?

—·—

Slavery was abolished in 1808, it got Abraham Lincoln assassinated for having too much humanity in his soul; "Thou Shalt Not Kill" didn't seem to help him.

So, while gun supporters are happy to quote a part of the Constitution from the previous century, why is slavery not resurrected as well?

Although would it not make sense, for the sake of empathy, if this time around the white people were the slaves?

Bought and sold like, say - guns?

Is this issue even remotely complicated?

Through which channels do weapons reach the hands of terrorists?

If it is not known, why hasn't somebody found out?

If it is known, why has it not been made known to everybody?

If it is known, why is it still happening?

Does anyone believe for a single moment that I, and billions of others, don't already know the full, detailed answers to those questions?

—·—

Why did an American President drop two atomic bombs on innocent Japanese civilians?

How are America accepted as the self-appointed judge of who should possess such devastating weapons?

......

Why is there money for missiles and weaponry, but none to house the homeless?

What is the root of this relentless fascination with killing?

Wars kill an awful lot of people, so why is war not always, without any exceptions, the very, very, very, last resort instead of an option that is always on the table?

Is it simply because of the fact that wars make a lot of money for a lot of people, while peace doesn't make any money for anybody?

Why is the functionality of the United Nations applied differently to different countries?

Why do some war criminals get prosecuted while others do not?

In particular, why do Western leaders have immunity from enforcement of UN international laws?
Why is it that when Western leaders want to perpetrate aggression, consultation at the UN is routinely bypassed?

There is not a single question within this passage that has a complicated answer.

That stink of the bullshit of hypocrisy is, once again, strong upon the air.

Too many things are valued above the lives of human beings.

....

And so the sacred Commandment has been adjusted to make it more workable for us and our 21st Century barbarism - it is implemented as "Thou Shalt Kill When There Is A Good Enough Reason".

Everybody seems comfortable with the update, especially with Propaganda there in place, to help people to see things correctly.

Watching the Television

One day,
instead of looking at the TV,
I looked at the TV.

I thought about the game shows,
that apart from Pointless, and Countdown,
and The Cube,
seem to consist of, and revolve around, answering
endless barrages of trivia questions.
Just too many shows to list by name. Hundreds.
I mean, the sheer innovation.
I guess that people sit in team meetings
and actually get paid to invent the
piles of vacuous crap.

....

Reality TV,
where dreams have become monetisable
commodities.

We start with 12 hopeful participants.
Each week the all-powerful panel of judges
boot somebody off.
Those super-suspenseful cliffhangers
as we hear who is going home.
20 seconds after the word 'is.......'
as the camera cuts from face to face
until it has shown every contestant,
and finally the name is uttered
and the axe falls on them.

The pure magnificent genius of the idea

has caused the propagation,
worldwide,
of that exact format.
It is so wonderful
that it almost makes me regret
that I chose to abandon access to terrestrial TV.
I looked at the singing talent shows –
first The X Factor,
and wondered where all the past winners are.
Be under no illusions,
the judges, and their egos,
are the real stars.
I wondered how angelic and
powerful the singing voices
of Simon Cowell, whose upper lip
no longer seems to move,
(I do hope that was the effect he asked and paid for,
Robbie Williams likewise).
of Louis "You made that your own" Walsh, or
of Sharon "I'm so proud of you darling" Osbourne are,
since these are all apparently singing experts.
Ayda Field is not a musician, she's just married to one,
does that count?
Apparently she is on the panel of Loose Women.
Does that count?
The X Factor is the brand name of televised karaoke.

Cover versions,
often of timeless classic songs that were written by,
and performed by,
brilliant singers and musicians,
given amateurish rearrangements and then
crucified by the twiddly-widdly vocal acrobatics
which, it seems, 'good singers' need to demonstrate
in order to triumph in the plastic karaoke contest.

211

It certainly makes every singer sound identical.
Each judge, also referred to as a 'mentor'
with an unusual,
different meaning of the word,
praises the contestants in their team
while criticising those in other teams,
usually saying "you chose the wrong song",
so one assumes they are experts on that as well.

The bland predictability of the
entire superficial circus
doesn't seem to matter.
The carefully stage-managed spontaneity;
"stop, stop, stop, sing something else".

A 'sing-off'
that need not even take place
because judges vote for their own
team member anyhow.
But one assumes that as long as the
phone calls come in
and everybody gets well paid,
that's all that's really needed.
I'm getting the hang of this capitalism thing.

I also observe that most of the winners,
and the many other non-winner
hopefuls that have the
virtually identical voices,
seem to fade away when the
competition ends each year,
despite having had months of primetime exposure
and the direction of an expert guru on top.
It doesn't seem to add up.
I think I can conclude that

212

wrecking other people's songs
is not a path to a meaningful musical career,
nor even to a meaningless one.

Conversely, on The Voice, the panel
are all able to sing,
which makes a little bit more sense I think, IMHO.

Britain's Got Talent is also always judged
by some of the most talented people on Earth.
Somehow they got the genius of
Amanda Holden and Piers Morgan,
the Creme De La Creme
of entertainment talent themselves of course.

I have decided to invent a talent show for sculptors,
judged by me.
I am not a sculptor,
having never sculpted anything in my life
after my efforts with Plasticine at the age of six.
I am therefore obviously well
qualified to pass judgement,
that seems to be how these things
are supposed to work.

I did observe that the talent show for budding artists
is judged by successful, professional, skilled artists.
How barmy an idea.
That will surely never catch on,
it's too weird a formula.

....

Then I thought about the soap operas.
Coronation Street, Eastenders, Emmerdale, Hollyoaks.

One or more of them

more or less
every single day
of every single week
of every single month
of every single year.

It is a brave person that does the math,
and calculates how much of their life
is spent in front of these productions.

I wonder if, on my deathbed,
I will be consumed with a frantic regret
that my life was wasted and ruined
because I spent my time on mountains,
or in forests, or deserts, or beside oceans,
hand in hand with someone I love?

Whether reading sublime literature or poetry,
appreciating music full of pure genius,
laughing and crying as hard as I could
at the sheer emotions resulting from
complete joy or complete sorrow,
was a wasted existence?

Because I chose not to spend
the large fraction of my time
that others did,
gazing with awe at countless hours
of Coronation Street, Eastenders,
Emmerdale and Hollyoaks.
How earnestly will I weep on that fateful day?
I'd have missed all those cliffhangers
that forbid you to miss an episode.
Who killed who?
Who cheated on who, and who with?

Will _____'s guilty secret be discovered?

I have a tip which might help any desperate addicts;
miss one episode, and the
second onward is a piece of cake.
In almost no time, freedom is delivered.

Those team planning meetings will still be buzzing
with the electricity
of super-creative plans
for ingenious, addictive plot lines no doubt.

……

Then there's all the sport.
They even give you football results on the main news
FFS.
Some cricket matches take five days.
Golf tournaments take four.

Watching those in their entirety
takes serious commitment.
Is snooker even a sport? What about darts?

The Olympic Games every four years,
is a veritable banquet of people
trying to win things
for the sake of winning things.
That at least is about
personal sacrifice
and the pursuit of excellence.

The Commonwealth Games though,
are subtly different.
Some countries are included
and others excluded from those,

215

on the basis of whether they have been
owned by Great Britain,
the so-called United Kingdom,
in the dim and distant past.

The term 'Commonwealth' is best understood
by going to the Tower Of London,
where you can see the Crown Jewels,
priceless gems stolen from other countries,
that belong to the
so-called United Kingdom now.
Should we give them back yet?
Invade.
Steal.

Common wealth!

There are the cooking shows. Where do I start?
On Masterchef, which is the one where each task
is referred to, and hyped up,
like it is a life-or-death challenge,
only half of the two judges is a chef.

The Great British Bake Off appears to be
the nation's favourite,
although people were
irrationally unhappy and alarmed
when a Muslim woman won the show.

Rampant racism doesn't need an actual reason.
The property shows.
The shows where people look around houses
and then not buy any of them.

Properties around Britain,

216

properties around the world.
Should our family emigrate or not?
Let's have programmes where people
buy cheap properties,
and then renovate them,
and then sell them,
and see how much profit they make.
Without a doubt, the original idea
will have come from a busy brainstorm
in one of those notorious team meetings.
Money and profit are always a safe theme.

…·…

Drama productions.
Either stories written long ago
where everybody gets to wear costumes from
bygone eras,
or angles on murder mysteries
solved by quirky, lovable detectives.

Then there's the news. Oh, the news.
We appear to tolerate
acute levels of patronisation.

We appear to tolerate
endless blunt efforts to manipulate us.
We listen to lie after lie after lie,
our intelligence insulted.
Who are the bad guys today
according to the editors?
Russia? Iran? Syria? North Korea? The EU?
Who are they saying are the good guys today?
Israel? Saudi Arabia? The DUP?
The British Government?
Do you see how carefully everything is worded?

217

Do you see through what is included
to what is not included?

Distractions, Distractions, Distractions.

Propaganda, Propaganda, Propaganda.

It is 2019, and Internet content is full of actual news.
Facts, expert opinions, intellectual dialogue,
not just doctored and edited and censored scripts.
You - we - I - get to look at all the views and angles,
and decide for ourselves what we think.
Hear both sides, hear every side.
The exact opposite of being
spoon-fed the butchered content.

…·…

People get bored
They get offended.
I used to get offended.
People initially scream at the screen,
and then they realise
that they have The Gadget.
There is a Gadget supplied with every TV
and it has immense power.
You point it at the TV,
and depending on which button you press
it changes the volume, the channel,
and, best of all, it
turns the boring, time-carnivorous machine
completely off.
That's a snippet of information
for those that complain
about what poor programmes
they have to put up with.

218

Your Gadget means you don't have
to put up with anything.
I used to use my Gadget quite a lot,
but at the moment I looked at the TV properly,
it was very simple
to make the decision
to cut television totally from my life.
Some five years ago or so,
that is exactly what I did.

Now, instead of the reality TV boot-off cliffhangers,
the game shows,
the singing talent shows,
the soap operas,
the sport,
the cooking shows,
the property shows,
the drama productions,
and, most profoundly and importantly,
the news that isn't news;
my life is now occupied with
Music, by musicians that can
sing, play, and write music.
Literature, though not celebrity autobiographies.
Movies.
Poetry.
And crucially of course,
when wanting information,
the Internet.
source of all types of information available.

I spend much of my time outside, in nature,
breathing fresh air, smelling the countryside,
awestruck by the beauty
of views from high up of valleys, forests and oceans.

219

Of standing beside towering majestic trees
or the simple wonder of a waterfall.
Walking barefoot on a beach,
or an expanse of grass.

And so, not surprisingly,
I have never regretted my decision for a second.
I had realised that what accesses my mind
is too important to delegate,
especially to people
that I have no trust or respect for.

There is no place for raw sewage in clean water.

I actually did take back control of my life.

All by myself.

The Will of The People? Brexit – The Last Word

There is much more content in my armoury about the whole issue of Brexit, the campaigns, the campaigners and their various lies and deliberately withheld omissions, the failure of engagement with intellectual arguments and debates in favour of sales pitches and slogans. From Project Fear to Take Back Control, neither of which contains a single number, timescale or specific fact. No information at all - and the other thing which had no specific detail included in it was the very ballot paper itself of course. Only Remain, or Leave. There is another entire book in my possession that only needs some editing. It will reinforce and expand on arguments introduced in this piece, greatly.

It is precisely because the ballot paper contained no detail, that whilst the 'snowflake' supporters of Brexit claim to be united, rallying increasingly around the "no deal is the best deal" ticket, in truth they had absolutely nothing concrete to hang their hats on from the minute the referendum result was announced. For a few examples, some Leave-voters wanted to keep Freedom of Movement, others didn't, others recognised it might be part of a compromise. The same with the Single Market and the same with the Customs Union. There was not a whisper in the entire Leave campaign about Ireland, which is logistically very tricky and very crucial, because it wasn't as sexy as "taking back control" (of things that we already had control of) which was deliberately hollow, and implied that the Leave option was easy and absolute when it was the exact opposite, it was always complicated, not to mention full of contradictions.

We did not hear a word about long and awkward negotiations being necessary from Messrs. Farage, Johnson or Gove, to inform their followers of the process that had to be navigated over (initially) a two year period, that turned out to become much longer. A transition period was added, and Theresa May's proposals would protract that further still. The absence of explanation of the negotiation process was about as conspicuous-by-its-absence as it is possible to be. It was implied that we, the so-called United Kingdom, held the advantages and the leverage when the opposite was true, the EU did. It seems very sensible and logical that since the voters were given nothing that could be called information, and that what they were given in place of that were a blend of outright lies and false implications, that the whole result should not really even be allowed to stand.

Adolf Hitler, of all people, who certainly knew how to use Propaganda, stated in his book Mein Kampf (My Struggle) that

"If you wish the sympathy of the broad masses, you must tell them the crudest and most stupid things."

He also said:

"All propaganda has to be popular and has to accommodate itself to the comprehension of the least intelligent of those whom it seeks to reach."

In hindsight, it is observable without any doubt that the Leave campaigners did exactly that, and Jacob Rees-Mogg has picked up the same mantle and is the loudest shouter of waffled nothings at the present time. No specifics, woolly rhetoric, avoids any numbers, facts and intellectual content like the plague. Everything is completely and utterly vague, and some of it is simply false. "Taking back control of our money, our laws and our borders", meant nothing whatsoever because we already had control of our money, our laws and our borders.

Of course there were all sorts of ventures that were shared and jointly administered with the EU, none of which encroached on our laws and our borders at all, and as far as money is concerned, apart from a notorious, crass and ridiculous statement on the side of a bus that not even the staunchest Brexiteer believed, the crunching of the colossal numbers of the pros and cons of EU membership contributions against the catastrophes of lost trade outside it, were not offered up properly by either side though at least the Remain camp did try, weakly and ineffectively. But any warnings were poo-pooed as Project Fear, however many senior economists, financial experts, intellectual heavyweights, business leaders and academics said it. You had to be pretty dumb to ignore the experts (even though Michael Gove told us

223

that people had had enough of experts - we were to consult mystics, soothsayers and hermits, or preferably Nigel, Boris and Michael, one presumes, since they are certainly not experts) but millions of stupid numbskulls bought the hype. The Propaganda had been accurately pitched and eagerly swallowed. Exactly as Adolf had explained it.

Ventures that the EU had involvement in, that involved money coming into the country rather than out, were a great many funded scientific research projects, agricultural subsidies, huge numbers of grants to local government initiatives, not to mention all the trade tariffs for the 44% of our exports that (used to) go to other EU member states. Our judicial system is fully intact, with the European Courts able to arbitrate on human rights matters for example, Theresa May of course giving speeches about human rights legislation needing to be abolished, which she U-Turned on of course. The EU are rather better and fairer with human rights anyway. Our laws, I am not sure which laws needed to be taken back control of, as all the Magistrates' and Crown Courts are doing what they have always done.

And a question is relevant here, which is........

Would the austerity-obsessed Conservative Party decide to suddenly cough up and fund all the EU-funded bodies with the £350 million a week - apparently later admitted to be an incorrect figure by any method of calculation - that we already know the NHS would have to whistle for and still not get?

The people that receive all of those EU monies are unanimous in believing that all of those grants would vanish. After all, there are corporations and billionaires to give tax breaks and incentives to, on the basis that they would then be able to "create jobs", which is in fact another myth. "Lie" is a more accurate word.

I have my own theory as to why David Cameron chose to grant the so-called United Kingdom the opportunity to stop being united and split itself in half. For what it's worth, my take on it is this; every adult in the so-called United Kingdom was given an equal vote, it was irrelevant what our IQs were, our academic qualifications, our sharpness of awareness and intellect. People from high-brow intellectuals to people that can barely read or write, all had an equal amount of power in the decision. I think that Mr. Cameron felt the result would be a safe vote to remain within the EU but called it wrong, because the fact that the referendum revealed to us was that 51.89% of Britons were just too gullible, and so voted for a result that better informed people instinctively did not vote for, with no need to listen to dishonest and meaningless sales pitches. It was so obvious that it seemed impossible that it could end any other way. To people with enough contextual awareness, it didn't seem possible that there would be enough people to deliver a result to leave. All credit to the combined Propaganda drive of Nigel Farage, Boris Johnson, Michael Gove and of course the priceless and earnest support of Right-Wing tabloid newspapers, because they did win, even though winning actually meant losing. And just look at the extent of the mess that has resulted.

I have lost count of the number of times that I have heard Nigel Farage bellowing (the only setting his voice appears to have) pompously about the "unelected bureaucrats of Brussels". It's utterly shameless of him, because he has been an MEP for very nearly 20 years, and although he knows full well that the EU Parliament, which is a fully elected body, is the only EU institution that can pass legislation, he misleads everyone about it at every chance he gets. The EU Commission, whose members are unelected, can only propose legislation for the Parliament to consider. Neither he, nor the fat oaf with the stupid hair, or the guy whose wife tells him what to do by email, though sending it to the wrong person, (Google the Gove) nor the Right-Wing Press, or the latest madly posh multi-millionaire that never shuts up with his tirades of drivel, told or tell the British electorate about that profound distinction. Why the Remain campaign did not highlight it is a complete mystery, other than that their sales and marketing skills were useless. But it is a perfect illustration of the factual and intellectual information that was deliberately distorted, and of course Propaganda is only effective if directed at the least intelligent people - here it worked perfectly. In Britain, we have a very similar set-up at the House Of Commons level, because the chamber is occupied by our elected MPs, and behind them there are a large number of civil servants, from the senior staff known as Permanent Secretaries, through entire departments such as the Home Office, the Foreign Office, the Treasury, the Department of Education and the Department of Health, and many others. None of them are elected, they are employed, and they play no part in passing legislation exactly like the EU.

The suggestion - and it was far more than a suggestion during the campaign, it was an accusation and a declaration intended to mislead - lie - to voters, that the EU was less democratic than the British system, was completely false. You can liken the EU Parliament and Commission to the House Of Commons and the appropriate departments staffed by civil servants, and to that extent the systems are similarly democratic.

However, that is by no means the entire picture, and since nobody had the courtesy to tell anybody within the campaigns, I will, years too late, explain.

Above the House Of Commons there is the House Of Lords, and that is full of unelected 'life peers'. Not all are life peers, but most of them are. The members of the House Of Lords are appointed to their seats by the Queen on the advice of the Prime Minister, it's all very, very cosy indeed.

This reminds us that above the House Of Lords we have our monarchy, and to describe that institution as being comprised of unelected members rather makes a mockery of the word itself. Unelected, unaccountable, unfair, un-anything that is remotely to do with the word 'democracy'.

So, not only was the complete and utter lie that the European Union is less democratic than the British Establishment deliberately told to the British people, but the proof that people believed pure rubbish and nonsense makes itself clear at the same time. Some sub-human tabloid readers, that clearly ask no questions of even the most ludicrous assertions and

227

take them as gospel, just went with whatever they were told. Ironically, some of those dim, mad people went absolutely ballistic at the "out-of-date-unelected-fogies" (their words not mine) at the House Of Lords when they started throwing out Brexit content. "Abolish the House Of Lords NOW!" was suddenly the outcry. One minute our democracy is second-to-none, the next it needs a total overhaul. The people that argue for Brexit contradict themselves with every passing minute, they can't make sense of anything, it's all way too complex for them to process, it's worse than understanding the 9x table. And each number in that has digits that add up to 9 so it's one of the simplest of the lot.

It's no wonder they were easy to convince, and it shows beyond any fragment of doubt, two things; one, the Remain campaign was asleep at the wheel to allow this to happen, and two, most profoundly, a few percentage points difference between people that voted for a pile of stupid lies and a slogan, and people that were able to understand the implications and vote intelligently and sensibly, is not acceptable. This is too big, and too important, to be decided in that way. There is too much at stake - the votes of England, London being the glaring and highly notable exception, and Wales are already causing Scotland and Northern Ireland to be forced out of the EU against their will. What definition of democracy are we following there?

It is apparently entirely legal, and therefore possible, for us to reject Brexit even now, and return to the top table of the EU instead of crashing out into oblivion, doubt and uncertainty. I keep hearing politicians say that it would "divide the country" to do it. Since the vote was virtually 50-50, once again blindness and verbal diarrhoea are in play. My very title says exactly that, and Brexit is a fiasco. Common sense is now overdue. Any course of action divides the country. We have a Divided Kingdom.

Something else affects things when one thinks of the bare scrape of a majority of three years ago, in a purely demographic frame. This is a very, very important point, which shows exactly why Brexiteers make so much noise about "respecting the referendum result" that again is repeated time, after time, after time, after time. Repetition persuades people, it's tried and tested Propaganda. The persuaders know it, newspaper editors know it in particular, and so once again, many Britons use the argument all the time with monotonous, tunnel-visioned stubbornness.

....

Now, here is a "Train Of Logical Thought". Remember we are talking about three years ago, and we are being expected to honour a 2% margin. 2%! Next to fucking nothing.

1) In that time frame, many of the oldest voters have since died. We know that a large proportion of them voted to Leave.

2) Lots and lots of the more open-minded and pragmatic-thinking people that voted Leave, realise they were hoodwinked by a sales pitch that had

nothing specific in it. That the Take Back Control assertion was about things that we already had control of. Just go to YouTube and find examples of James O'Brien of LBC, tearing apart people to give examples of stupid reasons given as to why they had voted Leave. A whole raft of people did not have any understanding of anything relevant whatsoever. The behaviour of Alexander Boris de Pfeffel Johnson, career politician, Eton-educated, Balliol College, Oxford (classics), who in his dulcet baritone recited Take Back Control of our money, our laws and our borders when we already had control of our money, our laws and our borders, and who would run around writing newspaper articles that seemed to rattle on about various unspecific boring waffle, but actually only really conveyed "I am determined to be the Prime Minister". Nigel "Foxhunter" Farage bellowing about unelected EU bureaucrats. Explosions and uprisings of poisonous, but reasonable-sounding statements like "we don't want to stop immigration, we just want controlled immigration" (you have to be a doctor, though even that isn't good enough for some people, who think that only a doctor trained in the so-called United Kingdom can actually practise proper medicine) or with no attempt at sounding reasonable at all and just going online to rant against Muslims, or immigrants (never using the word 'refugee'), or the EU negotiators, or any other EU state, or Angela Merkel. Whingeing that all migrants don't go to any other country than the so-called United Kingdom when it is a fact that we are not even in the Top 10 destinations.

3) In that time frame, a far larger number of young voters have reached voting age. The huge proportion of them, and the sheer numbers, far more than the Leave voters that died, constitute a colossal number of Remain voters. Why is that so? Why are they mostly Remain supporters? I could write another book about just that, perhaps I will. For what it's worth I'll supply some information. Youngsters think positively. Youngsters have open minds. Youngsters have a world view. Youngsters have no, or less, chips on their shoulders. Youngsters on the whole are not racists. Youngsters are computer literate which means they just click a mouse to make their vote. I don't need to explain the tsunami effect that has on the dynamic, the seismic shift to Remain. Only 2% has to be the swing. I do not need to say another single thing about it.

Since I have mentioned London, which as I just said tellingly voted Remain, it was wonderful to behold the London Eye lit up with the EU emblem on New Year's Eve. Online forums were full of racists spitting venom, they were livid. These are people who make no bones about despising Sadiq Khan, the Mayor of London, and that write hate-filled tirades that are full of spelling mistakes, words of one syllable, incompetent syntax, the punctuation of a toddler, as one has come to expect from them, whenever his name is mentioned. Apparently Theresa May can turn the Metropolitan Police budget into dust, terrorists can pop up at random and at will, and it's Mr. Khan's fault. Racism on the march, another excellent reason to reverse the decision if those are the kind of people that caused the stupid, crazy debacle.

Various other commentators didn't like the EU colours much, though in general they were commentators that usually write inconsequential dross. I think one of them might be a relative of my gold bullion adviser Hugo Double-Barrel. Judy Harley-Barley or something.

Obvious, but apparently necessary, empirical logic is required. **Londoners** voted **Remain**. The firework display was in **London**. Mr. Khan is the Mayor of **London**. So everything was aligned with the people of **London**. Please say that was simple enough. I also can't help imagining a little smile on Mr. Khan's face at the thought of getting his own back on a bunch of illiterate, nasty, xenophobic yobs. Respect is due to him. And it is time that our politicians made some proper decisions, perhaps demonstrating, just for a change, that however easy their degree was, however little experience of anything worthwhile they have, they are willing to grasp the opportunity right here and now to show some true leadership and do the right thing.

Apparently Article 50 can legally be revoked, and so either it could be done without fuss, or a 2nd referendum, that would be another inefficient and (again) expensive process, would demonstrate those points labelled 1-3 but far later. Why are governments always doing long-winded things? (Because it's not their money that pays for it all). And as for the EU? Well how on Earth we are worthy of their tolerance when they say that even at the last minute we don't have to crash out, that's incredible. After the way we have treated and spoken about them – not all of us of course. That is because they have integrity and honour way above ours. It shows the difference in the kinds of people that they are, and that much of the so-called United Kingdom now appreciate.

Theresa May was trying to convince the people and Members of Parliament of the so-called United Kingdom, which frankly has no chance in the foreseeable future of deserving the name, to accept a proposal which had a great deal in common with Remain anyway except that we would have absolutely no influence. It certainly does not resemble Leave, as Leave-voters are screamed from the rooftops.

It's got to the point where suddenly Leave voters and thick, useless and irresponsible politicians are now trying to puff their small, puny chests out and rather than lose face, claim that No Deal is the best available option, when it has always been, from the very start, the worst possible outcome of them all.

Jacob Rees-Mogg could do with explaining to his followers how he can say anything with any meaning to them, because he swims in an ocean of many millions of pounds and will not himself be adversely affected by us leaving the EU, while the companies that put food on their table might just disappear. The ports, like Dover, where people that need to use it are not just terrified, but absolutely certain, that things are going to grind to a halt, and the motorways will turn into miles and miles of lorry jams that will make 'Operation Stack' look like a trip to Eurodisney - by rail or air of course.

I have made my contempt for politicians in general crystal clear, but at least there are some, such as Nicky Morgan and Anna Soubry - Tories no less - acting with courage and brains on this matter. I am not going to name everybody in that group. But this is the time for our trusted representatives to act with a display of wisdom, strength and the leadership that they all think they possess but never prove. If there was a Cabinet, as I described before, that was comprised of real experts, for example from business, schools, the police, and other people that have high-functioning logical minds - scientists and mathematicians once again the example to quote - we would, I can say without the slightest trace of doubt, not be where we are. This is simple and not complicated. For goodness' sake do what you were elected to do! And stop worrying about your own careers and how you look - because a lot of you are not looking good anyway, that's for sure. Asking most politicians not to worry about their careers as priority one, well, it's certainly a massive ask, but it is that which most of the time proves why they are not suitable people to do that job.

And the Prime Minister, in an ideal Narniaworld, would be leading from the front in the **right direction for the**

good of the British countries and not worrying about how she looks, her despicable loyalties to the Democratic Unionists of Northern Ireland, and trying to sell a huge pile of horse manure which delivers nothing that either Remain-voters or Leave-voters want. Nobody wanted her plan. The MPs that said they did were only hoping for their loyalty to contribute to their own advancement, which is what bad politicians always do.

Cancelling the whole damned thing means that we stay at core of the EU, like we always have been, though there have constantly been dissenting, disruptive voices scheming in the way of proper functionality and trust. We would just have to try and forget that a vote for Remain in the first place would simply have meant carrying on as we were the following day and nothing would have changed, so all the wasted time, money and heartache would not have happened. We could have pursued reform of the EU from the correct and most influential position, I.e. INSIDE IT. We'd have been able to retain all the positives of EU membership and worked on the areas that needed it from within, and - of course - the Government would have been able to get on with doing some governing, just imagine the waste of so many peoples' time that has gone on. All the employees and administrators as well as politicians. An example of efficient governing would be ditching the stupidity and misrepresentations and negative economic effects of austerity, and to substitute it with a positive and progressive economic system. Imagine that.

Scotland and Northern Ireland at last would have their Remain votes honoured, and if we are extremely lucky they won't break from the Precious Union, though they can hardly be blamed if they do, the way they have been treated over this. They both voted to Remain, and they both did it by larger margins than the Brexit margin for the SO-CALLED UNITED KINGDOM.

Printed in Great Britain
by Amazon

33953708R00139